State and Evolution

State and Evolution

Russia's Search for a Free Market

YEGOR GAIDAR

Translated by
JANE ANN MILLER

University of Washington Press   *Seattle & London*

This publication was supported in part by the Donald R. Ellegood
International Publications Endowment.

Library of Congress Cataloging-in-Publication Data

Gaidar, E. T. (Egor Timurovich)
  [Gosudarstvo i evoliutsiia. English]
  State and evolution: Russia's search for a free market / Yegor
  Gaidar ; translated by Jane Ann Miller.
    p. cm.
  Includes bibliographical references and index.
  ISBN 0-295-98349-3 (cloth: alk. paper)
   1. Russia (Federation)—Politics and government—1991. 2. Russia
(Federation)—Economic policy—1991. 3. Soviet Union—Economic
policy. 4. Russia—Economic policy.

DK510.763.G3513   2003   2003050737
330'947'086—dc21

Contents

Preface to the English-Language Edition

THE BOOK HERE PRESENTED TO THE ENGLISH-SPEAKING READER WAS written in the fall of 1994—that is, before Boris Yeltsin's reelection to a second term, before the 1997 attempts to accelerate reforms, before the 1998 financial crisis, before the grand rise and fall of the Russian oligarchs, and long before Mr. Putin's election to the Russian presidency. When later it was suggested that I publish an English edition of *State and Evolution,* I felt a certain temptation to rework the whole book, to incorporate everything that had happened since its first publication.[1]

I eventually rejected the idea. *State and Evolution* is a work that stands on its own as part of Russia's ongoing process of comprehending her own history, of understanding her present and her past. "Updating" would be a mistake, in part because recent history seems to have confirmed many of the book's initial conclusions—first and foremost, that the crux of political conflict today comes down to the relationship between property ownership and government authority.

In the late 1980s the march of history turned into a sprint, as the Berlin Wall fell and the "velvet revolutions" of Eastern Europe took place, as the Soviet Union's socialist empire collapsed and the USSR itself disintegrated, as market reforms began and democratic institutions emerged—all in the space of a very few years.

State and Evolution reflects this sense of urgency, this sense that a particular kind of revolution was taking place. I am just as convinced now as I was then, in 1994, that the chief issue Russia is wrestling with today is this. What kind of order are we building? Where are we heading, as we come down from the "socialist heights?"[2] Toward a "Western-style market economy?" Toward nomenklatura capitalism?[3]

The difference between then and now is that *then* I assumed we could resolve these questions in a year or two, or three. Yet they are as problematic today as they were in 1994, and they will remain the nexus of Russia's economic and political battles for decades to come.

State and Evolution is devoted to the influence of history, and above all Russian history, on the present day. Understanding the extent to which the past continues into the present, understanding the meaning of the past, takes years. As we analyze the record of economic reform and of newly established democratic institutions in the countries of Eastern Europe, and as we analyze the enormous difficulties involved in promoting *both* in the newly independent states that have emerged from former Soviet republics, we inevitably come to the conclusion that our socialist and pre-socialist legacy still plays a pivotal role. When socialism collapsed in Poland, in Hungary, in the Baltics, an entire generation of people still remembered from personal experience what markets, market institutions, and private ownership were, what they looked like. In Russia there was no such experience to be had. In 1991, the vast majority of Russian citizens had never seen a normal retail shop, never touched a piece of convertible currency. But a market is first and foremost a set of historical traditions, of established norms of behavior; it does not spring out of nowhere.

The effectiveness of any democratic institution largely depends on the degree to which it is supported by a vital, self-sustaining civil society. Socialism always tends to suppress civil society, but the scope and severity of that suppression were never consistent across the socialist empire. So we should not be surprised that the emergence of democratic institutions in Poland, where even under socialism the Catholic Church and the family farm had remained relatively autonomous, came far more easily than it did in Russia, where civil society had been systematically and severely repressed for decades.

Another key factor that made the choice of an open market economy easier for many Eastern European nations was the consensus among their political elites on strategic economic and policy issues. Restoring the artificially ruptured connection to the West, to Europe, as quickly as possible, becoming full-fledged members of the European community and eventually members of the European Union—these were the goals of the political elite in Poland, Hungary, Czechoslovakia, and the Baltic states. And these goals strictly limited their freedom of choice in setting economic and political policy. The understanding was this: if you want to become part of Europe again, you had best conform to European standards on property rights, on fiscal and monetary stability, on transparency in government spending, on banking regulations, on democratic institutions.

In Eastern Europe these standards thus became the framework for the new forms of social organization that followed the fall of socialism. In Russia, however, things stood quite differently. Our society was deeply divided over the fundamental question of which path Russia should choose. Where should we go from here? Should we immediately try to turn ourselves into a normal European state? Or should we try to resurrect our old fearsome empire? Hence the enormous disagreements over strategic economic and political questions, hence our long-standing political instability, our zigzags in economic policy, our continuing inability to effect needed structural reforms and build workable market institutions.

In the latter half of the 1990s, the stalemate between President Boris Yeltsin, who was convinced that Russia must become a free-market, democratic state, and the parliamentary majority, who dreamed of restoring the empire, made it virtually impossible to implement any consistent or considered policy. Reforms ground to a halt, as a dangerous compromise between soft budgetary policy and a hard-line monetary policy paved the way for the financial crisis and crash of 1998.

As I reread *State and Evolution* today, I see obvious traces of my own internal debate over whether the events of 1990–93 constituted a true social revolution in Russia. As the saying goes, sometimes you can't see the forest for the trees. Now . . . I see the forest.

In the last ten years, a full-scale social revolution has indeed taken place in Russia. All the characteristic signs are there. Political institutions and economic relationships have changed radically. Deep differences of opinion on fundamental issues of state and social organization have come to light, both within the elite and throughout society at large. A war over redistribution of property has broken out. We have witnessed all the government weakness and incompetence, all the political and financial instability typical of such periods.

All revolutions are caused by one thing, i.e., by the sclerosis of existing institutions, their inability to adapt to change, to reshape themselves. The Russian revolution of the 1990s is no exception. But what made this revolution different was the fact that it was the first major revolution in a highly industrialized society. And therefore it was marked by less violence, by limited application of force, by wide-ranging compromise with elites of the previous regime.

And sooner or later all revolutions end in some kind of stabilization. Society can stand only so much chaos and unpredictability, and soon polls begin to show that people's first priority is "reestablishing order." A consensus grows, as does a readiness to accept a new reality and build on the achievements of the revolution. When in late 1998, thanks to a Communist majority in the Duma, the Primakov government came to power but made no move to dismantle market institutions, and when in the December 1999 elections all the political parties with any chance at all of gaining seats in the Duma wrote platforms favoring markets and private property, it became clear that Russian society had reached this basic consensus.

Yes, of course there are and will continue to be fierce battles over how property should be distributed. There will be arguments over what form our market economy should take. But the fact of a market itself is already taken for granted. The frail state, the weak government—dictated by the very nature of the revolutionary process rather than by this particular policy or that—are ceding place to strong government. A tired society is ready to allow its new leaders a wide range of action, a greater amount of discretion.

The question that concerns all of us is how our leaders will use that discretion. In England, for example, only after the revolution of the seventeenth century did a full-fledged system of protections for private property come into being, a system that eventually laid the ground for the industrial revolution and two centuries of English dominance on the world stage. In late eighteenth-century France, postrevolutionary stabilization resulted in a government that dragged the nation into protracted wars of conquest. In twentieth-century Russia, Stalin used this postrevolutionary period to reenserf the peasantry and forge a rigid totalitarian dictatorship.

Symptoms of the political ambivalence typical of postrevolutionary stabilization are being felt in today's Russia as well. On one hand, this new consensus gives the government a new opportunity to set considered, useful policy aimed at resolving problems that in past years were deemed unresolvable, and so were never confronted. On the other hand, there is the very real danger that strengthening official authority will lead to the rise of yet another nondemocratic regime, that stabilization will foster the growth of authoritarianism.

"Social fatigue," discreditation of revolutionary values, and a certain nostalgia for the symbols of the old regime are hardly unique to late twentieth-century Russia. World history suggests that the end of a revolution does not necessarily mean the end of reform. All dogma to the contrary, revolution is not inevitably followed by counterrevolution or reaction. We use the term "postrevolutionary stabilization" in place of either of those to suggest that Russia has reached a kind of plateau, a place where she can take a deep breath, get her bearings, and decide where to go next.

What was the revolution of the 1990s for Russia? Was it a hard but salutary road toward the creation of a workable democracy with workable markets, the path to the twenty-first century? Or was it the prologue to another closed, stultified regime marching to the music of old myths and anthems? Let us consider how these possibilities played out in real politics, in the first year of postrevolutionary stabilization.

THE ECONOMY. Here we see obvious signs of an upswing: rapid growth in the gross domestic product, in manufacturing, in investments, in real income. There is much discussion around the reasons for this improvement: does it have to do with ongoing economic reforms, or is it conditioned solely by the devaluation of the ruble and the high price of oil? I would like to maintain that the current upswing in the economy has nothing to do with either. First of all, the new set of reforms launched in 2000 did not produce any real results until some time in 2001. High prices for oil of course favored economic growth, but can account for only 50 percent of the growth in the Russian GDP. Finally, there was a time (1991–94) when the real exchange value of the ruble was immeasurably lower than it is today, and at that time what resulted was not an economic upswing at all, but a drastic downturn in production.

In fact the explanation lies elsewhere. Over the last few years, we have reached critical mass: we have seen the creation of a sufficient number of well-managed, market-oriented companies capable of ensuring normal production through resources freed up from the inherited and inefficient Soviet sector. This process has moved slowly, burdened by problems left over from Soviet days and by the weakness of economic policy, but it *has* moved. And now, finally, we have an opportunity to use this foundation to foster economic growth.

Russia's economic downslide has lasted a long time, much longer than Eastern Europe's. But it has finally come to an end. Still, we should not assume that this in itself guarantees that sustainable growth will follow. Today's Russia still lives with the difficult legacy of the Soviet Union and the years of transition that followed its collapse. The experience of other nations has shown that under such circumstances economic growth can be fleeting and unsustainable. One crucial precondition for sustainability is the maximum use of current opportunities to resolve crucial structural issues so that reforms can move in a key direction.

One of the most important and positive developments in 2000 was that the Putin government demonstrated both the political will and the courage to not only draft a program of far-reaching structural reforms but to actually begin implementing it. Yet it was in this very year that the government ran up against a major psychological obstacle. The fact is that high oil prices made everyone complacent. Imposing rigid discipline when you have neither money nor choice is easy enough. It is much harder if you have at least some of both. Reforms are a product of necessity; they go forward when there is no way to go back. But Putin's government has not succumbed to the temptation of quick and easy solutions, and that instills a certain optimism.

Perhaps the most significant event of 2000 was tax reform. This was a subject much discussed while Yeltsin was in power, but at the time it had no political support. Now it does, and in 2000 a number of important steps were taken: one was the introduction of a "flat tax" on personal incomes; another was the abolition of the turnover tax.

But this is just a beginning. In short, tax reform will be a long war on many fronts. Nonetheless, one positive result is the very fact that we have moved in a key direction—one that promotes the expansion of a real and open economy and a corresponding shrinking of the shadow one.

Significant progress has been made in establishing fiscal federalism. Over the 1990s, a rather complex and conflicting system of resource allocation and spending authority throughout various agencies had developed. But the measures taken in 2001, which include a complete transfer of value-added tax revenues to the federal budget and of income tax revenues to regional budgets, have evened out regional income and created a more reasonable budgeting system throughout the government.

Notable progress was made in efforts to standardize customs fees and duties and in fact to lower them overall—a very important step in the integration of Russia into the global economy. However, progress in reforming the banking system, in consolidating property rights, and in reforming natural monopolies has been limited at best.

FEDERALISM. The second area in which Russia has made significant progress is the restructuring of federal institutions. This has included the creation of federal districts and reform of the Council of the Federation. However, the results are mixed.

On one hand, these changes were absolutely essential. How can there be any real federation if its component states do not enforce federal law? How can there be a real federation when regional governments limit trade between regions? If the enforcement of federal law depends entirely on the whim of some local official (or some federal official, for that matter), then there is no federation. In that sense, the steps recently taken to create a single, unified system of government in Russia are logical, natural, and right.

At the same time, precisely because we are in the midst of postrevolutionary stabilization, movement in this direction involves a great deal of risk. The danger is that in its eagerness to reinforce "the vertical" (the chain of command) Moscow will lose all sense of proportion and begin interfering in what are by law purely regional and local matters.

Still, the very fact that today's Russia is a real, if imperfect, federation testifies to the success of recent developments.

Governing a federation is obviously much harder than governing a unitary state, and the obvious temptation is to find some "easy solution." But Russia can only be a true democracy if she is also a federation of truly local government and regional governments; she is far too diverse and complex for anything else. Any attempt to reestablish a unitary state would be a terribly harmful and dangerous idea.

MILITARY REFORM. In the year 2000, the government took what are in my view some very positive steps in this area. The most significant of these was the decision to make large-scale reductions in troop strength over the next three years, to 2003, and to use the funds freed up by these cuts to address social problems facing service personnel, to improve the quality of military training, and to ensure that our forces have modern weaponry.

DEMOCRATIC RIGHTS AND FREEDOMS. The dangers characteristic of postrevolutionary stabilization have manifested themselves most markedly in issues touching on the work of democratic insitutions and the protection of real freedom of speech. Here the risk of losing the ground gained in the 1990s is greatest. Our bad old habits acquired over centuries of pre-Soviet autocracy and decades of Soviet rule incline us to this, as does the loss of faith in democratic principles and values.

The ideology with which many Russian politicians are now flirting comes down to "we don't need democracy, we'd rather have a Russian version of Pinochet; the hell with democratic freedoms for now, let's create a working market economy first." Such an ideology is both extremely naive and extremely dangerous.

We live in the twenty-first century, after all. It is a century of rapidly changing global conditions, when how many factories you build is less important that how you react to the challenges of a changing world. Democracy is hardly a perfect instrument, but it is a far better means of adapting to the world than any other, far better at ensuring flexibility and effective response. Any undermining of the democratic institutions for which we have paid so dearly would be a terrible tragedy for the country. We would eventually have to recreate them anyway, and it would once again be difficult and painful. Russia would end up paying twice over for what has already been bought at great cost.

History has seen a number of examples of nations building an effective market economy before they created democratic institutions, but there is little likelihood that Russia could restage this scenario for herself. Our traditions of authoritarianism, imperial rhetoric, isolation, and state corruption are far too closely intertwined. In Russia, the struggle for a market economy and the battle for an open society and sound democratic institutions are indivisible from one another.

The more than a decade that has passed since the collapse of the Soviet Union has convincingly demonstrated that there are two roads out of the "Second World" of socialism: one leads to the First World of states with established democracies, with working market economies, with a high standard of living; the other leads to a Third World of persistent poverty and corrupt authoritarian regimes.

The baggage of tradition makes our crossover to the First World difficult and exhausting; it would be all too easy for Russia to get off the track. Time will tell whether or not we can make the transition. We need to realize that the difficulty of the mission is no excuse to simply throw up our hands in defeat. It is merely a reason to try harder.

State and Evolution

1 Two Civilizations

East is East
And West is West
And never the twain shall meet.
—Rudyard Kipling

I

THE SOUND AND FURY OF 1987–91 HAS SUBSIDED, AND WE NOW REAL-
ize that reducing the historic collision of forces in Russia to "a basic
confrontation between capitalism and socialism" is hardly an adequate
description of what took place during those years. At the time, the main
thing was to pronounce socialism in Russia dead, to state loudly and
unequivocally that our future lay with the market—but we cannot stop
there.

There is no denying that the vast majority of countries that currently boast a capitalist, market-oriented economy (or the rudiments
of such) are hardly prosperous. In fact, many of them are plagued by
poverty and economic stagnation. Most of them are far poorer than
Russia, a country still new to markets. Yet these countries do have their
millionaires—as do we. So it turns out that rejecting socialism does not
automatically guarantee either general economic prosperity or a decent
standard of living—something that many Russians counted on in 1990,
when they naively assumed that all we had to do was trade one fetish
for another, a Communist birthright for a capitalist mess of pottage,
Das Kapital for capital gains.

The fact is that far more people inhabit the poor and dejected Third

3

World than the prosperous First. Moreover, the doors of the socialist Second World open into both. Critics of capitalism—"Russian patriots, Communists," and their ilk—are absolutely right in noting this, but the trouble is that their plan for preventing Russia from slipping into the Third World, their prescription for her assumption of her proper social and economic place among nations, is completely cockeyed.

Russia's current historical dilemma comes down to one of the fundamental dichotomies of world history: the traditional confrontation between East and West that existed at least until the so-called awakening of Asia in the late nineteenth century. Since that time, many Eastern countries (including the "easternmost" of all) have made skillful use of selected Western principles of social organization. These are the very countries that are prospering today.

Of course, a work of this small scope cannot pretend to describe global historical processes. Historian Arnold Toynbee designated twenty-one civilizations in the history of man, twenty-one types of social organization, only two of which might be termed "Western." And even if one accepts Toynbee's classification system, the remaining nineteen can hardly be characterized as "Eastern." That is, the key features, the system-defining elements that I intend to apply in this work, when speaking of "Eastern" as opposed to "Western" civilizations, are more narrow and localized in nature. And while these criteria may not be applicable to the entire range and diversity of historical phenomena, they are absolutely crucial in any attempt to define the overall development of both society and state in Russia.[1]

The concept of an "Asiatic mode of production" is still relevant to Russia, because, unfortunately, Marx's analysis all too accurately reflected Russian realities of the day. His analysis was grounded in traditional European denunciation of "oriental despotism," as Europe strove to define itself as "not the East." Marx saw the absence of private property in the East as "the key to the Eastern heavens":

> If it is not the private landowners, but the state itself that stands in direct opposition . . . to manufacturers/producers[,] . . . if the state itself is the owner and proprietor and also the sovereign

power, then rent and taxes are essentially the same thing, or rather, taxation does not exist apart from rents . . . The state is here the ultimate landowner. Thus sovereignty is simply landownership on a national scale. In this case there is no such thing as private ownership of land, although private and/or communal holdings and land use do exist.[2]

Obviously, then, landownership lies at the heart of property relations. Societies in which there is no true private ownership, in which property ownership and government authority are joined at the hip (but where the latter is the dominant twin), in which official ties and relationships are the coin of the realm, the gauge of any and all societal relationships, societies where a bureaucracy rules both economic and political life—these are classically "Eastern" societies. Such features are typical of Third World societies even today, and are the chief cause of backwardness and of chronic poverty. These features also serve to ensure that the backwardness and the poverty will continue to exist, to perpetuate themselves, to take root and spread.

Deep-rooted, too, are the historical reasons for this.

The infinitely diverse non-European ancient and medieval world found certain concepts generally alien, among them clear-cut guarantees of private ownership or civil rights, and the notion that the state exists to serve society rather than society the state. The Eastern state might tolerate private property and markets, but that was all. Property and markets were always suspect, always strictly controlled and directed by an omniscient and ever-present bureaucratic apparatus. Requisitions, seizures of property, loss of social status or title, restrictions on consumption of luxuries might be the lot of even the wealthiest property owners in a despotic regime, should they fail to cultivate their government connections. In such regimes, both past and present, the state is all. It is both the key to the good life and the only reliable protection against poverty. Lose your position—lose your estate. Property is the natural prey, and the state is the natural predator, always in pursuit, always redividing and redistributing existing spoils.

Law codes of Eastern empires were usually long, detailed enumerations of the many and various obligations of imperial subjects; they were lists of administrative restrictions on people's lives and work, with only scattered references to these same people's right to own anything at all.

"Strong state—weak people." This phrase, coined by Chinese legist and reformer Shang Yang in the fourth century B.C., is the epitome of the Eastern governmental ideal.

But a strong state may pay dearly for having a weak people. Any system in which property and official authority are indivisible—in which, moreover, authority is primary, and property secondary—has certain distinguishing features.

In the first place, such a system provides no incentive for anyone to produce anything, or indeed to engage in any economic activity at all. Entrepreneurs who have no guarantees, who are always dependent, always worried over how to bribe or whom to bribe, are much more likely to turn to trade, to speculation, shady dealings, or outright usury (anything liquid, anything with a quick turnaround) than they are to put their money into long-term investments. Moreover, in this system the head proprietor (the bureaucrat) is nothing more than a parasite; that is, he is neither competent to deal with the complexities of running a business nor is he financially interested in its success.

This leads to economic stagnation and recurrent poverty, and hence the need for a "mobilization economy," an economy that has no incentives to sustain itself, let alone move forward—an economy that in fact moves only when prodded and poked by someone "up there." If left to itself, its forward movement soon grinds to a halt. And in order to restart the process the state must expand once again, reinforcing itself at the expense of the private sector.

In the second place, when political crises or transfers of power take place, a major redistribution of property almost inevitably follows. In this system property is, after all, merely an attribute of political power. Those newly come to power hasten to grab the property commensurate with their rank. And when significant property cannot be acquired without significant office, the very scent of acquisition can be enough to set off a political crisis. New powerful groups and powerful leaders alike may be ready and eager to storm the gates of government (often by piling up enough corpses to get over the wall) less for reasons of policy or state than for crudely mercantile ones masked by one form of demagoguery or another.

Hence property relations are as unstable as political relations. Official position becomes doubly attractive; first as pure power, and second as the only reliable source of wealth and material comfort. Thus a political crisis can end in a breakdown of the entire social and property structure. All this taken together serves to retard development and send the given society into yet another round of stagnation and poverty. And the poorer the society is, the richer its leaders seek to become.

In the third place, upon examination, even the strongest such state proves to be internally weak, eroded, eaten away by "state servants" hungry for gain.

Ordinary corruption soon leads to extraordinary wealth. Officials intuitively seek to solidify their own position, to convert official authority into material property. Soon holdings awarded for loyal service can be inherited; soon thereafter they can also be sold. And the moment the central state begins to weaken, its appointed servant begins to behave like a sovereign prince. Lands that formally belong to the state, lands that are meant to supply the state with whatever it might need, are in reality bought, sold, and controlled primarily by civil servants.

"L'état, c'est moi." This is in fact the bureaucrats' true motto, their definition of privatization. Put tax money into your own pocket; treat state property as if it were your own. This is bureaucratic privatization.

This sort of privatization corrupts and weakens a state, of course, but by no means changes it into a different *type* of state. Government officials remain government officials. They have no intention of "seceding" from government and taking "their" property with them. The entire purpose of Eastern bureaucratic privatization lies in one thing: to satisfy, within the framework of the existing system, the voracious appetites of those in power, to do so by maintaining the indivisibility of property from the always dominant state.

Given this sort of "perestroika," true and legitimate private ownership never evolves into a social institution. Instead, state officials merely redivide the spoils among themselves. The vicious cycle in which Eastern civilization revolves is never really broken. It merely begins a new round. The state, riddled from within, eventually collapses. And whoever the new head of state might be—the strongest among rival officials, or the leader of a peasant revolt, or a neighboring ruler bent on conquest, or a nomad invader—that ruler once again restores central authority, redistributes private holdings, and tightens controls over land use. He replaces the defeated vassals with his own appointees. State revenues increase. But then, a generation or two later, his appointees begin privatizing state property. And the cycle begins again.

Chinese history, of course, provides that most vivid examples of this dynastic cycle. But the pattern is obvious in ancient Egypt and in Central and Western Asia as well.

This pattern offers the entrepreneur or proprietor little, if any, hope. For when the empire is expanding, growing stronger, the property owner is always suspect, always subject to strict controls, constantly at risk of having his property seized. Any weakening of the empire opens the door to chaos, to civil strife, looting, foreign invasion. A strong and despotic regime is dangerous. A weak and despotic one is unendurable.

The very notion of reform in the non-European ancient world was inextricably bound to the idea of restoring the decrepit house of state— rebuilding on old foundations. This meant tightening controls over landownership, making the bureaucratic machine more efficient, putting pressure on those groups that the state had not yet swallowed completely—nobility, landowners, property owners.

Eastern civilizations predate Western ones. Ever since the days of tribes and clans, some official authority has played a crucial role in the establishment of order in any human group. A certain relationship between the rulers and the ruled arose long before either side began to accumulate property or even think about property relations. In human history, power and authority have always been primary, and property secondary. The very acquisition of property has been made possible in large part because those in power have structured and organized human communities and what they do. It is only natural that property relations should arise as some part of an already established "power matrix."

By firmly subjugating property to government authority, Eastern societies (by which I mean, again, a general structural model rather than specific laws or dynasties) achieved a certain stability. Not until the end of the nineteenth century, perhaps, did change begin in earnest, as very different civilizations met, joined, and clashed.

2

The Western system branched off from the Eastern in the second third of the first millennium B.C., in Greece. This so-called Greek miracle remains a riddle, as prominent Oriental scholar L. Vasiliev notes: "It is difficult to say exactly what brought about this revolution in the archaic world—something we can confidently liken to a social mutation, since this was the only such revolution in all of human history, a revolution unique in both its character and its consequences."[3]

Not until the nineteenth century did East and West truly meet. This encounter demonstrated the superiority of the Western system, as all movement went in one direction—at least until Japan and other dragons of the East had assimilated enough of the Western system to begin to compete with it.

What was the essence of this "Western mutation"? We can judge to some extent by looking at works by Western scholars who have noted, with some surprise, that the very cornerstone of Western institutions—the notion that private ownership (of land, for the most part) can exist independent of the state—is a concept lacking in the East. Hence, the essence of the "Greek mutation," the very thing that sets it off from its Eastern progenitors, is a change in the concept of property relations; it is the emergence of a highly evolved private property system seen as legitimate not only in juridical terms, but in social and psychological ones as well, a system increasingly independent of the state, one in which ownership is truly a private and personal matter rather than an attribute of official position. Today, when such relations seem patently obvious, we may be surprised at how weakly they are represented in Eastern societies. As Vasiliev notes:

> One thing is certain: the chief result of this structural transformation [i.e., of traditional societies in ancient Greece—Ye. G.] was that property relations, a concept hitherto unrecognized or undeveloped elsewhere, especially when combined with a

market dominated by private production of commodities and private slave labor [i.e., individually owned rather than state owned slaves—Ye. G.], began to take center stage. Moreover, the stage was not a powerful, centralized state, but a small self-governing community, a city-state, or polis. Thus after Solon's reforms (in the early 6th century B.C.) a structure built upon private property arose, a structure found nowhere else in the world.[4]

As a result, a system gradually came into being wherein the state was not the master of the polis, but the instrument of the polis. The notion that citizens of the polis possessed certain inalienable rights became axiomatic. Of course Greece and Rome alike saw their share of tyrants, of brute force and arbitrary confiscation, but these were only ripples atop a powerful wave, a current of individual rights and relations. What in the Eastern world was natural law, a natural perquisite of power, was seen in the West as tyranny and arbitrary exercise of power.

Even when the Roman Empire fell to barbarians— conquerors who turned an entire system of established property relations and individual rights upside down, who laid waste to highly evolved social and governmental institutions, who imposed traditional Eastern models at sword's point—the legacy of the classical world did not disappear without a trace. It survived, at least as an intellectual tradition, to eventually, slowly, stubbornly modify feudal institutions and feudal law, to give privatization an ideological base.

The European feudal system that arose out of the ruins of Rome was, unlike Rome itself, not unique. A tendency toward feudalization when central authority grows weak is characteristic of the ancient world. If no powerful central bureaucracy exists, lands are divided up among warlords, who then strive to convert these conditional holdings into permanent ones. Tradition aids them in this endeavor. The prince appointed to administer a certain territory gains a measure of independence; his children gain the right to inherit. The village next to a knight's castle gains some defense against bandits and marauders, because the local lord is far more likely to come to the villagers' aid than is some faraway king and his army.

Private ownership of land in the Roman or contemporary sense of the word did not exist, could not exist, in the Middle Ages. King, duke, lord, village, and peasant all had overlapping claims to the land; all considered it rightfully theirs. Similar structures can be found in China in the Zhou and the Warring States periods, in Fujiwara Japan, in many other parts of the world and many different eras.[5]

What truly sets Europe apart is the centuries-long stability of its feudal system, and the centuries-long weakness (or perhaps the flexibility) of the European state.

From the tenth century, once the last great wave of unrest and migration set off by Magyar, Moor, and Viking conquests had subsided, a fragmented, decentralized, stable feudal state was to remain the norm in Europe for hundreds of years. Dynastic wars began and ended, scores of kings and feudal barons came and went, but none of these events were truly earthshaking. That is, they did not uproot social institutions. They merely pruned the tops. The losing side was not slaughtered wholesale or shipped into slavery en masse. A war did not require that a society exhaust all its resources, or wholly submit itself to the state in the interests of national survival; war did not mean that all property rights must be given over to the sovereign.

In general, then, political upheaval in the West was far less likely to lead to the total substitution of one property-owning social group for another, to a total redrawing of the property map.

A single feudal family might control the very same lands in the fifteenth century as it had in the tenth. However, in terms of mentality and behavior, the feudal lord of the thirteenth century was no longer the barbarian raider his ninth-century forebear had been. By now the life of his family had long been joined with the life of his peasants, a life rooted in customs, habits, and traditions that governed both peasant obligations and peasant rights. As John Stuart Mill said: "Custom is the most powerful protector of the weak against the strong."[6] This is how the foundation of a society is gradually laid, through this sense of the legitimacy (or the lack thereof) of any given action by either an individual or the state. Legitimacy breathes life into written laws; it makes them more than mere pieces of paper, and in doing so turns a violation of law into something morally questionable and dangerous. Were it not for the concept of legitimacy, society would indeed be merely a Hobbesian arena for a war of all against all.

In Europe, throughout all the turmoil, private property and private property relations remained a legitimate concept. Custom may have been a keeper of the old ways, but it was also a mechanism by which property relations were transformed and changed. That is, if a peasant's duty was clearly defined, why not, as the European economy moved away from natural exchange, deal in money instead of in-kind payments or labor? The state ceased to redistribute lands already held and, as time went on, the crown's claim to any lands outside the royal family's own desmesne grew weaker. Manor lands were divided by long-standing custom into those held in tenure by the peasants and those belonging directly to the lord. Here and there, short-term cash rent became a common practice; later, such agreements would become long term. "The commons" gradually became individual holdings. Lords became landlords; servants became tenants.

By the century, English freemen had gained the right to sell land without asking the lord's permission. The custom took root, and the overlapping rights of feudalism gave way to individual property rights.

The very fact that the European feudal state was not all-powerful is precisely what gave birth to Europe's complex, differentiated civil society. The medieval church was never subordinate to the state; its powerful hierarchical structure had survived the fall of Rome, thus creating alternative paths to social advancement and limiting the absolute rule of secular monarchs.

Trading towns that had sprung up under the patronage of a monarch or a seignor, towns that had initially been protected by his forces and fortresses, soon acquired, a life, a hierarchy, a government of their own. These cities bore little resemblance to their Eastern counterparts, most of which remained under rigid state control.

Here and there, dormant classical institutions—Roman law, private property, civil rights and freedoms—began to send out new shoots. Feudal society would begin to rediscover them as a centuries-long process of evolution finally created the social base they required.

Property and state diverged, split, and ceased to be indivisible by definition. Property, now sacrosanct by custom, was no longer arbitrarily confiscated. The loss of a powerful state position no longer meant the loss of one's property. Moreover, the furious development of private enterprise—in trade, for the most part—made it possible to be rich without being in government. The increasing sophistication of markets provided additional guarantees against abuses by the state, against arbitrary seizure of property. Montesquieu was among the first to note that the capital outflow was putting limits on absolute rule.

The now-established custom of separating property from official position paved the way for a more complicated social structure, for a multitude of hierarchies existing outside the hierarchy of the state. There was the state itself; there was the hereditary aristocracy; there were landowners, towns, and town dwellers (the bourgeoisie); there was the church—all functioning as independent but closely intertwined forces. This is precisely where the prerequisites for accumulation of hereditary wealth and creation of private capital came into being:

> Society accepted the phenomena that preceded capitalism at the point when it [society] became more or less hierarchical, and thus fostered the continuity of genealogical lines and the sort of long-term capital accumulation without which there would be no opportunity at all. It was necessary that inherited wealth be passed along; that inherited wealth increase; that profitable alliances be formed; that society divide into groups, some of which would dominate or have the potential to dominate; that society be graduated, where social ascent might be at least possible, if not always easy. All this presumed a lengthy, very lengthy, maturing process.[7]

The greatest stimulus to innovation and productivity is protection of property rights. Once those rights were guaranteed, fifteenth-century Europe ever more confidently took a path of economic development—which would soon outstrip population growth.

3

It is particularly important that we fully understand the role of the feudal state in the genesis of European capitalism.

We have already noted that European socioeconomic progress was a product of weak states. Yet should it not be the state that ensures the preservation of tradition, the opportunity to peacefully accumulate wealth, to just as peacefully transfer it from one generation to the next? Should not the state be the bulwark against arbitrary redistribution of property? Should not the state be the first line of defense, not just against foreign predators, but against its own predatory vassals?

How can a society resolve vital issues like this in the absence of a powerful state? Just how catastrophic a weak state may prove to be is all too obvious. We have only to look at the history of the Rzeczpospolita Polska for an example.[8]

But history has given us an answer to this question. In the East, the state "protected and defended" society by turning society into a part of the state, or rather, by refusing to allow society to develop on its own, by covering it, smothering it, crushing it under a protective shell.

In Europe, where the physical survival of ethnic peoples was never in question, a unique situation arose. European societies began to change and develop faster than states did. What emerged was an elite (some of it hereditary, some not) that felt itself independent, that saw itself not as a cog in the state machine, but as a fundamental and necessary part of the social system. Yes, a strong, inflexible state can in theory guarantee private property rights; it can provide protection against a whole array of enemies—feudal lordlings, rival states. But the cost of such protection is enormous. The state is too powerful a protector, one that gives property owners no protection against the most terrible, most powerful, most ubiquitous enemy of all—itself.

Societies had first to become strong enough to accept, without fear, such a protector as this. Only a society with established traditions (including a tradition of rule of law) and highly developed social differentiation, with a deeply rooted belief that people and property exist independent of the state, a society with institutions that safeguard such independence, would be ready and able not only to withstand the heavy hand of government, but to use that hand in society's own interests. If property ownership is defined and made legitimate through the state alone, there can be no such thing as a market. If such legitimacy is not contingent on the state, if private ownership is primary and one's relationship to the state secondary, then the state itself will work for the market, will become its instrument.

The emergence of powerful nation-states in Europe, where the social ground was already prepared, was not a matter of predestination. It was no sudden miracle. Social development and the emergence of markets had provided the impetus for national unification and, over time, helped to dismantle an increasingly shaky feudal system. These nation-states—sixteenth and seventeenth century England and France, seventeenth and eighteenth century Prussia—grew up and out of their societies rather than being set atop them like so many gigantic idols.

Economic policy in European states was always active rather than passive, and only in rare cases was this policy ever purely fiscal. In some sense "state capitalism" is less characteristic of the twentieth century than of the seventeenth and eighteenth, when a policy of "state mercantilism" aimed at fostering initial capital accumulation dominated the West. It was the state, after all, that sought trade, that established colonies, that went to war over both; it was the state that underwrote the East Indian and West Indian companies in England and France respectively, that built navies (and in the nineteenth century, railroads), that helped create an entire industry devoted to national defense, and so on and so on.

All these state efforts went with, rather than against, the natural course of market development.

They played out on a strictly defined field of private ownership and free markets (albeit that freedom was limited by protectionist tariffs), of separation between private ownership and state ownership. Within this framework, the state did not trespass on "private holdings," and thus worked to foster capitalism rather than suppress it. European states deftly adapted to market conditions, easing state pressure when private capital became strong enough to sustain development on its own.

Western European societies thus managed to find the most effective solution so far to the crucial problem of how best to combine tradition with development.

In the East, systems remained rigid and inflexible until they finally collapsed in blood and violence—only to be restored unchanged. In the West growth was based on tradition; growth reconciled contradictions, and summed up the material and spiritual experience of previous generations.

This is no apologia for the West. Western societies have had their share and more of crisis and turmoil, and we do not know what troubles may await them. The modern Western system of government has any number of inherent flaws and injustices; it is hardly the last word in human wisdom or some "happy ending" to the history of humanity. Capitalism is not the final incarnation of the absolute historical ideal. No doubt as the world becomes more integrated, new forms of society, new ways to live together will eventually develop. As Winston Churchill so aptly said, democracy is the worst form of government—until one considers the alternatives. And indeed, of all the civilizations that have played a part on the world stage in the last few centuries, Western civilization has been the most effective actor.

The most dangerous challenge ever faced by European capitalism has come from within. In the eighteenth and early nineteenth centuries change had come gradually, slowly. Subsequent technological progress and social-political upheaval drastically accelerated its pace. By the mid-nineteenth century, the European ship seemed to have gone off course, sailed into a storm; European history seemed to be caught in some fatal, "dialectical" maelstrom. Hence Marx's ominously solemn, "Mephistophelean" pronouncement: "Contemporary bourgeois society . . . , which has created, as if by magic, such potent means of production and exchange, is like the sorcerer who can no longer control the otherworldly forces he himself has summoned up by his spells." Some lines later, even more ominously, solemnly, dialectically, he continues: "But the bourgeoisie has not only forged the weapons of its own destruction, but has given birth to the [very] people who will wield those weapons against it—today's workers, the proletariat."[9]

As we well know by now, Marx's analysis of capitalist society led him to all the wrong conclusions. He believed that bourgeois production relations lagged behind the actual forces of production. But in reality, the storms that raged over Europe for a good hundred years, whether they were called "socialism" or "communism" or "fascism" or "nazism," those storms that seemed to indeed uproot the tree of European civilization, were a product of something entirely different.

4

Urbanization and the breakdown of a traditional way of life had laid the groundwork for a revolution in the hopes and expectations of the still impoverished lower classes. As class barriers fell, the idea of equality for all took hold of the masses, and took on the force of a battering ram. Yet the proletariat itself was less swept up by this idea than were the "Rastignacs" of the day—ambitious but marginalized young men who saw no opportunity to capture their "rightful" position by climbing the social ladder. Their only option, therefore, was to knock the entire ladder to the ground and kick it to pieces. As the Communist anthem "Internationale" proclaims, "We shall raze this world by force / and build a new one over it / Who once was naught / Will now be all."

Actually, I fail to see what is so proletarian in those words. Above all, this was an anthem to and for the young and ambitious. It is no coincidence that the leaders of the most destructive revolutionary movements of modern times—Marx, Bakunin, Lenin, Trotsky, Mussolini, Stalin, Hitler—were all typical representatives of a "homeless" intelligentsia, men who had not yet found their place in the sun. Of course I would not want to equate a major thinker and brilliant man of letters like Marx with a criminal like Dzhugashvili or a paranoid madman like Schicklgruber. But the three do have one thing in common: they all, on some level, belonged to a marginalized intelligentsia.

H. G. Wells, for example, wrote quite bluntly that while he had little sympathy for Marxist theory, which he found "incredibly tedious," and that although he had long had the urge to arm himself with razor and scissors and write a piece called "Shaving Marx's Beard," he certainly sympathized with Marxists, very few of whom had ever read *Das Kapital* cover to cover.[10]

Rapidly expanding and seemingly inexhaustible opportunities for manufacturing, set against a social backdrop of persistent poverty and growing inequity, highly organized production processes set against an obviously chaotic market (a combination leading to mass unemployment on the one hand and overproduction on the other) provided a natural breeding ground for a variety of anticapitalist ideologies that attributed all of contemporary society's woes to the existence of markets and private property, and all saw hope for a "bright future" in the elimination of both, in the "socialization" of production. The most sophisticated, finished, and intellectually attractive form of anticapitalist ideology was Marxism, and it spoke directly to seemingly obvious truths, presenting its followers with a whole and complete picture of the world. It combined the persuasive authority of rationalism with the moral messianism of a secular religion.

And so, the European crisis was a crisis of technological progress, a matter of change outstripping tradition; it was a crisis of hope, of too great expectations, when the customary poverty and disenfranchisement of certain groups "suddenly" became intolerable. What Marx thought was a crisis in production relations themselves was not that at all; it was a full-out assault on the legitimacy of those relations.

The crisis was least pronounced in the very citadel of capitalism— England. One would think that here, of all places, it would be most acute, since here production relations were most advanced. But that was not the case. The crisis in bourgeois consciousness in Victorian and post-Victorian England, *Forsyte Saga* England, was relatively mild compared with that on the Continent, precisely because in England the idea of individual freedom and the sanctity of private property had far deeper roots.

In any case, the very backbone of European civilization—the centuries-old belief in the legitimacy of private property ("the sacred right")—was being subjected to a furious intellectual and emotional critique by people who with "fatal conceit" (hence the name of Nobel prizewinning economist Friedrich August von Hayek's book) were drafting their own blueprints for a "new society."[11] Traditional, hierarchical, private-property-based society suddenly seemed outrageously unjust. Now envy became legitimate; indeed envy was no longer envy, but "righteous indignation" justified by the desire for equality, which then evolved into the assumption that "surgical" methods could legitimately be used to redistribute wealth. Among reactionaries this process was sometimes translated into local terms, switching from the Marxist mainline onto a racist, national-chauvinist sidetrack (don't rob all the rich, just the non-Aryans).

5

And how did the West respond to the Marxist challenge? The irony of history (one of Marx the Hegelian's favorite terms) is that history seems to have played no favorites, and to have turned against Marx himself. Marxist theory was not some fatal dose of cyanide administered to an ailing West. It was a vaccine.

Instead of mechanically suppressing Marxist opposition, capitalist societies began to assimilate it (sometimes to the counterpoint of anti-Marxist rhetoric). This assimilation was painful, of course. At the end of the nineteenth century and the beginning of the twentieth, Western society went through an agonizing mutation, but came out of it alive and well. The much anticipated "decline of the West" (anticipated by Fascists and Communists alike, not to speak of free European intellectuals) never came to pass.

Two thinkers—Eduard Bernstein and John Maynard Keynes—played a leading role in beating back Marx's revolutionary challenge.

In *The Preconditions of Socialism and the Tasks of Social Democracy,* Bernstein laid out a theory of socialist reform far more threatening to orthodox Marxism than any "exclusionary laws against socialists" enacted in Germany at the end of the nineteenth century. Bernstein opposed violence and revolution to a process of ongoing social compromise by means of which democratic societies' most rampant injustices might be redressed. His conclusion is expressed in his famous aphorism, one that helped take considerable steam out of the Marxist movement: "The end itself is nothing, movement toward it is all."[12]

With the turn of the century, capitalism took on an increasingly socialist bent. Class barriers were breaking down (while in "real socialist states" they were being reinforced in truly feudal fashion); both theoretical and actual equality before the law was becoming a reality—not through revolution, but through continuing reinforcement of democratic traditions. The ugliest forms of injustice were beginning to disappear. Universal suffrage was becoming the norm. Labor laws were being created to protect the rights of employees. Systems providing for unemployment compensation, pensions, and government provision of education and public health were beginning to take shape.

Equally important were changes in economic policy.

It was John Maynard Keynes, of course, who best expressed the essence of these changes. Marxist revolution was giving way to Keynesian evolution.

His book *The General Theory of Employment, Interest and Money* was published in 1936, when the world was just beginning to emerge from the Great Depression, the greatest crisis capitalism had yet undergone— a crisis, moreover, that was playing itself out on a stage where the USSR's "planned socialist economy" seemed to be enjoying brilliant and indisputable success, and where Nazi Germany's "planned economy" was booming.[13] The Keynesian version of free-market capitalism advanced both general economy theory and spoke of specific measures aimed at reducing unemployment, increasing real buying power, and overcoming the economic crisis—all without doing away with private property. This led to much more effective state regulation of the economy. And while Marxist economic theory was laced with some universal human urge to destroy, Keynesian theory was not. It was reformist and pragmatic, with a rather impressive array of practical tools at its disposal.

Keynesian economics found their reflection in President Franklin Delano Roosevelt's New Deal. In the midst of crisis, faced with massive unemployment, this American administration decided to forgo certain principles of classic capitalism and significantly increase government involvement in the national economy. This decision helped save the day. Later, something like the New Deal also found its place in postwar Europe.

Today, some fifty or sixty years after the New Deal and the heyday of Keynesian economics, we have a better understanding of the significance of the mutation undergone by capitalism in the first half of the twentieth century, as it became less classic, and more socialist. There were two prerequisites for this change: one was the spiritual and intellectual crisis brought on by the First World War (which challenged the legitimacy of capitalist institutions themselves); the other was the economic crisis that rocked the world in 1929.

"The socialization of capitalism" actually proceeded along two lines that sometimes converged, but more often than not ran counter to one another. The first line was sociopolitical: elimination of legal privileges reserved for the upper classes, expansion of the social and political role of lower-status groups, institution of a wide array of social guarantees, including medical care, education, employment, pensions, et cetera, all of which would be supported by taxes, and the introduction of progressive individual taxation that included a tax on inherited wealth. The second line was economic: an activist budget and monetary policy aimed at managing overall demand and employment.

Today we may say with some certainty that the socialization of capitalism saved Western society, and it did so by leaving the latter's most crucial, systemic features—the legitimacy of private ownership, markets, the separation of property and state—virtually untouched. It left traditions relatively intact instead of slicing them up with the scalpel of leftist or rightist extremism. The New Deal made it possible for the "American automobile" to navigate safely through the very dangerous 1930s, to steer clear of Communism on one hand and National Socialism on the other. "Quasi-Marxism" worked to protect the West against genuine Marxism; reformism was a defense against revolution and totalitarianism.

Once the market was saved, and the legitimacy of private property maintained, the defense mechanisms of a self-sustaining economy began to do their work.

Yet while government regulation and social reforms may keep the underclass from exploding in rebellion, they do not lead to economic progress in and of themselves. Quite the opposite, in fact. The results of prolonged and consistent application of such policy are all too apparent: stunted economic growth, recurrent budget crises, inflation, reduced private investment and poor return on government investment, capital flight, and ultimately, economic stagnation and widespread unemployment—precisely those things that Keynesian policy was meant to combat.

And so in the 1970s the pendulum of Western economic policy began to swing back toward traditional capitalist values, toward economic liberalism and free markets. One way in which this swing expressed itself was the rise of monetarism, a legitimate heir to classical economic theory that gained political support as the so-called conservative wave of Western politicians (most notably, Margaret Thatcher and Ronald Reagan) came to power in the late 1970s and early 1980s. There was mass privatization of state industries; a war was declared on inflation.

Without going into great detail, I must say that no politician in his right mind will ignore other people's experience, nor will he automatically imitate it in order to "get a good grade" from the Chicago school of economies. Accusations that we were merely replacing one dogma with another, substituting monetarism for Marxism, were nothing but demagoguery. I remember all too well Ruslan Khasbulatov trying to stir up controversy at the Congress of People's Deputies. There are two vastly different concepts of a market economy, he said. One was the heavily taxed but "socially oriented" state (i.e., the Swedish model) and the other was the classic capitalist, laissez-faire state (i.e., the American model). He, Khasbulatov, firmly supported the former, while Gaidar was clearly a proponent of the latter. So, he said, deputies had to make a choice (apparently right then and there, by voice vote) of which path Russia should take.[14]

In intellectual terms this was ridiculous; in ethical terms it was outrageous. Even if we ignore the rank ignorance of such comparisons (for example, the "socially oriented" economy of Germany is much more strictly based on monetarist tradition than is that of the United States), it would be silly (let alone sad and embarrassing) to even pose such a question.

That is, be they Keynesians or monetarists, "socially oriented" states or "classic free-market" states, liberal, conservative, or social democratic—all these governments belong to a single global tradition. All inhabit a socioeconomic space based on the separation of state and private ownership, on the legitimacy of the latter, on respect for human rights, et cetera. Our first task is to enter into that space, and establish ourselves there. And then we can argue about models all we like.

The real choice facing Russia today is something else entirely.

A full century and a half separates "classic" capitalism from twenty-first-century capitalism. Russia is proposing to make its entrance onto this new stage of capitalism, not the old one. The role we play on this stage depends entirely on us, on the policy Russia chooses to pursue.

The question is not *whether* the state should intervene in the economy or not; the question is *which set of rules* should govern that intervention. That is, what sort of state do we want for Russia? As long as our "Eastern" tradition of "statism" continues unbroken, we cannot even speak of intervention at all, because this sort of state is built not to intervene, but to suppress. We already know what such a choice would mean for Russia: economic stagnation and an inevitable drift toward "Third World nuclear power" status. And therefore we will fight any attempts to turn our economy into some new variation on Marx's "Asiatic mode of production" that will turn Russia into yet another version of Marx's "Asiatic state."[15]

2 A Catch-up Civilization

Obedient slaves and lackeys,
we held, we were, the shield between two warring
races—Europe, and the Mongols!
—Aleksandr Blok

I

"CATCH-UP" IS A WORD THAT MAY BE APPLICABLE TO RUSSIAN CIVI-
lization, but not to Russian culture. European culture, especially since
the late nineteenth century, has been tremendously and fruitfully
influenced by Russia's great literature, theater, art, and music. Probably
one of Russian culture's great strengths lies in her East-West dualism,
in the clash of cultures. This dialogue between East and West has been
crucial; it has broadened our cultural space, it has created new reso-
nances within it.

But politics and economics, governmental order and economic activity, are another thing entirely. Here Russia, for many centuries, has been
a civilization constantly playing catch-up. In other words, East is East
and West is West. This is the history of Russia, the greatest Eurasian
empire the world has yet known.

Russia "stormed into Asia" (into Siberia, actually) in the sixteenth
century. Asia, however, had stormed into Russia and set up camp a full
300 years earlier. The whys and wherefores are obvious enough: our
country had always tended to serve as a shield rather than a bridge
between the two. As we know all too well, Russia's "uniqueness" arose
out of a multitude of factors: the schism that divided a once unified

Church into Roman Catholic and Eastern Orthodox (the latter heavily influenced by Byzantium); the enormous distance separating Russia and Western Europe; the enormous distances and sparse population within Russia itself; poor communications throughout. But the primary factor, the deciding factor, was the Steppe, and the nomadic peoples who inhabited it.

This is not the time or the place to discuss the rich history of the Eurasian Steppe. Only one aspect of this history has been truly crucial in determining Russia's socioeconomic development, and that is the history of conflict and confrontation between the nomads of the Steppe and the agriculture-based empires of the East. Nomads were the predators of the ancient and medieval world. Like arctic wolves stalking the oldest and feeblest members of a reindeer herd, they preyed on empires weakened by internal strife and conflict, by bureaucratic privatization, and often enough they brought entire dynastic cycles to an end. Each such conquest involved more than merely looting cities and trampling irrigation systems. Each incursion also brought about the total destruction of social institutions, of traditions of property ownership; each brought about a redistribution of both land and chattels.

The "island of Europe" was washed by an Eastern ocean on three of its four shores: Rus' was bordered by the Steppe and the Golden Horde, Austria by the Ottoman Empire, Spain by the Moors. Such dangerous proximity produced similar results in all three states: militarization of the society, fortification of the state as a bulwark against the East, bureaucratization, and delayed development. But Russia, in light of her particularly dire situation, ended up paying a much higher price than other border nations. The enormous mass of the Steppe set the trajectory of Russian history and to a great extent determined the social structure of Muscovy. Russian thinkers have long considered both the Tatar invasion and the "Asiatic spirit" that subsequently informed Russian bureaucracy—the "khan autocracy"—Russia's greatest misfortune. (As Aleksei Tolstoy wrote with angry irony, "You've gorged yourself on Tartary, and now you call this Rus'.") We should point out, however, that even those who considered "Tartary" the chief source of Russia's historical woes never couched this in ethnic terms—that is, Russia has never suffered from any sort of "tatarophobia."[1]

But whatever emotions might swirl around this issue, the facts are more important. In places where East and West actually met, social institutions of both types existed side by side. While Western influence may have prevailed in culture and ideology, economic and political structures more often conformed to Eastern practice. Moreover, such influences were never simple and direct; it was never a matter of simply imitating Tatar-Mongol models of political hierarchy or property ownership. Here, the complex and often paradoxical logic of history came into play.

In terms of landownership, even in the thirteenth and fourteenth centuries when the Tatar yoke lay most heavily on her shoulders, Russia was still moving (albeit somewhat behind the pace) along on the same track that European feudalism had.[2] The history of Volhynia and Galicia, western Russian princedoms pulled into the Lithuanian-Polish orbit in the fourteenth century, demonstrates where that path might otherwise have led.

The historical paradox here is that throwing off the Tatar yoke would, in the end, cost Russia more than enduring it ever had. The monumental effort required to free herself was precisely what sent Russia on her long journey down the "Eastern track."

Russia's fragmented feudal state had no time to develop into a whole one; the caterpillar never had time to grow into a beautiful butterfly. There was no opportunity to build a state based on private ownership and markets and the economic power those markets might create. The war against the Steppe forced the society to mobilize all its forces to the utmost, and to one end.

Under Ivan III, Vasily III, and Ivan IV (i.e., in the years when decisive victories over the Golden Horde were being won), the Muscovite state suddenly grew immensely stronger, but it did so at the expense of both the cities and the old boyar families.[3] Land grants were not gradually becoming permanent private holdings, as they were in the West; instead, the old system of conditional, *pomestye* holdings was being reinforced.[4] The state scrupulously controlled all distribution of property. This was the era in which Moscow brutally crushed Novgorod, a principality where ever since the eleventh century and the days of Yaroslav the Wise, any prince judged unfit to rule had been subject to expulsion by vote of the assembly of nobles, the Veche, and where even during Tatar rule, trade with the Hanseatic League and the very character of the city itself had fostered an independent economic life and a skeptical attitude toward established tradition. Now influential townsmen were being sent into exile, their houses and possessions confiscated and handed over to Muscovites. At the same time, peasants all across Russia were being enserfed in ever greater numbers, bound ever more closely to the land by edicts such as the abolition of St. George's Day, and Boris Godunov's ukaz of 1597.[5] The Church, too, was losing its autonomy, becoming part of the state machine. No wonder Stalin was so enamored of Ivan the Terrible; he admired not only the "Russian Nero's" general sadism, but also his governmental policy. Dzhugashvili could quite justifiably have traced his own "state genealogy" back to this tsar who raised the prototypical totalitarian house of state atop the bones of his own subjects.

In the Muscovy of Ivan the Terrible we find all the classic features of Eastern despotism. But Ivan's personal ferocity is not the point. His contemporary Cesare Borgia committed quite as many crimes as Ivan did. So, slightly earlier, had Richard III of England. Yet their kingdoms bore little resemblance to Eastern regimes, while Muscovy was coming to look more and more like the Ottoman Empire under Suleiman the Magnificent, or the Iran of Abbas I.[6] In these latter two we find the same sort of *pomestye* system, the same sort of state controls over distribution and redistribution of lands, over trade, over towns, the same absolute disenfranchisement of royal subjects, up to and including the tsar's own retainers. More important, though, is what we do *not* find, and that is true private ownership of land.

As all this was transpiring, rapid territorial expansion had begun. Russia was moving eastward over the Urals into Siberia and the Far East. But these territorial gains (the last of which were made in 1945) merely forced Russia into the "imperial trap." With every new expansion, new territory had to be defended, maintained, settled, exploited. This drained strength from the metropolis, as Russia herself gradually became a captive, a colony, a hostage to a military-imperial system that styled itself the savior and benefactor of its subject nations, the guarantor of their very existence. The Tatar yoke was gradually being replaced by a bureaucratic one. And lest popular rumblings against the exorbitant and never-ending tribute demanded by the state turn into mass revolt, the state began to cultivate a siege mentality, a great-power complex, xenophobia. The state was becoming sacrosanct, and so was everything connected to it.

Thus the state became a spiritual category, the object of a scrupulously maintained cult. In essence, the Russian state has always propagated a single true faith, a narcissistic cult of itself and of a "Holy Russian Empire." This was true in the era of official Orthodoxy; it was true in the era of official atheism. Aleksandr Solzhenitsyn defined this essentially pagan cult best when he said: "Writing the word 'God' with a capital letter is by no means required; writing the word 'government' with one is."[7]

Of course one should not go to the opposite extreme, and try to deny that there were times when the very existence of Russia was truly threatened (the Time of Troubles, for example). But these threats were not the only reason, nor even the real reason, that the Russian state was becoming stronger, truly all-powerful, crushing society with its immense weight. The Russian state had long since begun to exist for itself alone, and the self-sustaining state was crippling property relations and squeezing the life out of what might have been a self-sustaining nation.

As Nikolai Berdiaev so rightly wrote:

creating, maintaining, and defending the state has always been the sole and overwhelming focus of Russian history. The Russian people has had little time or strength left over for a free or creative life. . . . Classes and estates have been too weak to play the same role they have played in the history of Western nations. The individual has been pressed down by the enormous weight of the state, by its unbearable demands. Bureaucracy has grown to monstrous proportions. The Russian state . . . was forged in the midst of war—first war against the Horde, then war in the Time of Troubles—but always amidst foreign incursions and invasions. Thus the state became a principle, an abstraction sufficient unto itself, living its own life and acting according to its own laws, refusing to be part of the life of the nation.[8]

On its road to territorial, social, and psychological expansion, the mighty Russian state rolled over social institutions like a heavy wain, crippling them or sometimes crushing them entirely. As a result, the groundwork was never laid for a complex social structure based on private property and protection from the arbitrary exercise of power. The cult of the state warped the mind of the nation; it created a whole array of complexes that to this very day keep us from looking at our world, and ourselves, with a clear and rational eye.

2

It soon became obvious that as Russia was busy fighting off her enemies to the East, she was falling catastrophically behind the West—most obviously and alarmingly in the area of national defense. Victory against the Golden Horde was followed by defeat in the Livonian Wars; Poland remained an ever-present threat.[9] By the sixteenth century, Russian civilization found itself constantly struggling to keep up, a predicament that has lain at the heart of its problems ever since.

There were two ways to respond to the Western challenge. One was to try to achieve Western results without duplicating Western institutions or the social structures that had produced them, to do it all the "Russian way"—which meant relying on the power of the state, putting the spurs to a docile populace, squeezing out all its resources, forcing it to make a great leap, to make up the distance.

Ah yes—Russia is truly unique among nations. She was among the first "Eastern" nations to come into contact with the West. She was the only one that, without adopting "Western ways," was able for centuries to "almost catch up." Of course this was all achieved at enormous cost, and even then only in selected areas, ones in which all the nation's resources were concentrated. (But this in itself was a miracle: imagine Volga barge haulers yelling heave-ho, sprinting, and for one short stretch pulling side-by-side with a steamer.) Only a truly rich nation could afford that. But in the twenty-first century this sort of miracle may no longer be possible. If real reform is not begun, let alone finished, if we do not

choose a different strategy, we will fall behind once again. And this time
we may never catch up.

The other possible response was to restructure the entire socioeconomic system, to begin peeling away layers of newer tradition so as to
restore the older, interrupted one, i.e., Russia's social and cultural unity
with the rest of Europe. To switch tracks, to cultivate something like
European institutions, but to cultivate them in Russian soil, to let them
mature and then use them to nourish development, innovation, entre-
preneurship, economic growth. But all this inevitably would mean the
"taming of the state."

The struggle between these two alternatives has defined Russian
history for the last 300 years.

Peter the Great's policy was a peculiar mix of both alternatives, but
in the end, one that relied mainly on the power of the state machine,
on coercion. Tsar Peter had no intention of relinquishing power; the
thought never entered his head. Instead, he sought to expand the state,
to use it as a tool, his main tool, for solving the problems of the nation.

Europe has its manufactories and its mills, thinks Peter. Russia must
have them too. But in Europe these manufactories have grown out of
cottage industries and crafts, out of wealth accumulated over time, out
of the initiative, enterprise, and the labor of free men. In Russia, none
of this exists. You can't make something out of nothing, thinks the
tsar—at least not overnight, or even in a year, or two, or more.

Then again—perhaps you the tsar, the state, can force that growth.
You can give factory-owners a free work force by binding serfs to factories instead of landed estates. You can set peasants to work in factories instead of fields: x number of households work the forges, x number
work the furnaces. You can raise tariffs and customs fees; you can guarantee that only state-sanctioned manufacturers will hold a monopoly
on Russian industry.

But the disadvantages of this particular method of industrialization became evident as Russian manufacturing soon found itself at a
dead end. Moscow merchants complained of the poor quality of serf-
produced goods, of prohibitively high prices; they begged for permission to trade freely with foreign suppliers. A state inspection of factories
in the 1730s revealed that many Russian factories were nothing but

phantom enterprises existing only on paper, and that their proprietors were simply using the benefits and privileges of a crown patent to line their own pockets.

The crown's reaction to this situation was typical of "statism" at its most consistent: an ukaz issued in 1744 declared that "for poor quality of wares and lack of zeal in production, certain proprietors would henceforth be excluded from the official list of manufacturers."

The most graphic testimony to the nature of Peter's modernization efforts was an increase in the already burdensome cost of government. As early as 1680, the expense of maintaining an army and a navy was weighing heavily on our still underdeveloped nation; by the end of Peter's reign the cost of both had grown fourfold, as their budget share went from 50 to 65 percent. The overall cost of government also rose from 4.5 percent of the budget in 1680 to 10 percent in 1725.

Hence came changes in the tax system. An individual tax *(podush-naya podat')* was introduced, and by 1724 it was producing five times the revenue that the old household-tax system *(podvornaya podat')* had brought in. There was also a drastic expansion in indirect taxation. Ever since the Tatar-Mongol invasion, the Russian state's main means of mobilizing resources had been a tax on peasant communes, based on the principle of *krugovaya poruka,* a practice that had long impeded economic development in rural Russia. Given the enormous tax burden, given the fact that *krugovaya poruka* regularly allowed this burden to be shifted to the hardest working, most prosperous members of the commune, the government had no reason to change anything at all. It had no incentive to do so. Nor did it have much opportunity. And so the commune tax served to keep agriculture—the very foundation, the basis, of the nation's economy—in an artificially preserved and backward state.[10]

However glorious the military and technological achievements of Peter's reforms might have been, they were also a testimony to the self-destructive nature of Russia's response to the West. A powerful state, high taxes in general and overtaxation of the peasantry in particular, and the custom of *krugovaya poruka* all served to slow economic development. The natural consequence of Russia's enormously costly economic leap, during which time she lost up to 20 percent of her population, was further loss of ground to Europe.

Yet one aspect of these reforms remains attractive even now. This was Peter's emphasis on a common cultural heritage with Europe, as European influence on Russian social and cultural norms increased drastically. Yes, Peter's cultural reforms were imposed from above, and yes, they were just as crudely and coercively enforced as all his others. But paradoxically enough, the end result was that his crude and coercive state forced the creation of social groups independent of itself. None of this happened overnight, of course, but it did happen rather quickly, within a generation or two at most. European influence nudged Russian nobles toward greater independence, as they gradually claimed and won new rights and freedoms vis-à-vis the crown.

Thus a civil society at least marginally independent of the state bureaucracy began to take shape in Russia. Russian aristocrats of the eighteenth century felt much more at home at the court of France than at the Ottoman Divan. European influence also made itself felt in a broadening notion of civil rights (which at the time meant the rights of the nobility) and the inviolability of property rights (here again meaning property held by nobles).

Yet a fundamental split underlay the building of post-Petrine Eurasian Russia. It is a dichotomy that persisted throughout the eighteenth and nineteenth centuries, and we carry it with us into the twenty-first. Making a virtue of necessity, we proudly speak of Russia's "singular destiny," of her "messianic path." The fact is that this path has been no path at all. Rather, it has been the absence of one, the inability to choose which path to follow. Tsarist Russia fell into the chasm between the two. So did the Soviet empire. And yet here we are, building the new Russia directly over this fault line.

We have always been so busy duplicating European forms (especially the most superficial ones) that we have ignored what shaped them in the first place: a market relatively unfettered by state or bureaucratic dictates; a tradition of free-market, private property relations. At the same time, we have never quite managed to sustain our own "Asiatic mode of production." And so Russia's East-West society has lived in a permanent state of crisis.

After Peter, the crisis was everywhere. Russian bureaucracy took on its own peculiar form, combining the worst of both worlds. Russia absorbed Western (primarily German and Prussian) bureaucracy's coldness—its mechanical formality and absolute distance from the people it served—but neglected to adopt its preciseness and attention to detail. From Eastern bureaucracies came a spirit of petty tyranny, laziness, sloppiness, and of course the eternal scourge of Russian institutions—systematic corruption.

The Russian body politic was pathologically ill, a structure and a system completely out of balance. One has only to look to Palace Square in St. Petersburg: a vast expanse of flat stone, with a towering vertical column shooting up through its center. No gradations, no transitions, none of the normal, gradual steps that lend stability to a society or culture.

Russian peasants and the nobles seemed to live in two different countries; they literally spoke and thought in different languages—the peasants in Russian, the nobles in French. Today, only in Third World nations does this sort of social structure still exist. Yet the aristocracy was not yet part of civil society, a class independent of the state. In the eighteenth and nineteenth centuries Russian social institutions changed very slowly, and only with great difficulty did they gain some measure of freedom from bureaucratic control. The process remained unfinished even as late as 1917, although of course by that time tremendous progress had been made. In the second half of the nineteenth century and the early part of the twentieth, something like a civil society had almost managed to establish itself: Russia had a socially and materially autonomous intelligentsia, a "middle class," an entrepreneurial class, all of these socially and materially independent of the state—a union of the best and brightest among the gentry, the raznochintsy, the merchants. But this cultural veneer covered only a small part of the society; it was thin, and brittle, and cracked all too easily under the stress of the violent social collisions of the early twentieth century.

Property ownership (especially landownership) and property relations were even more complicated.

Throughout the seventeenth century property relations had been generally stable, although hardly very efficient. They were still grounded in the *pomestye* system, which was in fact a system of universal service, the enserfment of the entire population to the state. For the nobles, this meant obligatory military or civil service; for the peasants it meant taxation and tribute. The concept of private ownership did exist, but only as the barest germ of an idea; all lands belonged simultaneously to the tsar, the nobles, and the peasants. All claims overlapped. Of course here, as everywhere else, the system was evolving toward privatization: nobles who had initally held land under condition of service now sought to own it outright, to make it inheritable, to expand their rights of ownership. But there was also a countertrend at work, a trend toward greater state control over the granting and redistribution of lands.

At the beginning of the eighteenth century, Russia's rediscovery of European history and tradition was a powerful impetus toward privatization. But out of the complex mesh of interlocking claims, the crown chose only one link, found in favor of only one claimant—the *pomeshchik,* the lord of the manor. And to the surprise of the overwhelming majority of the population (the peasantry), the gentry were awarded *all* rights to ownership.

The revolution in agricultural policy that had begun with Peter's 1714 ukaz on primogeniture (which gave *votchina* and *pomestye* lands identical status) continued with Anna Ioannovna's ukazes of 1731 and 1736, Peter III's manifesto on the freedom of the nobility, and Catherine the Great's 1785 Charter of the Nobility, bringing Russian property relations into line with Western practice—in form, at least. But in fact this set of reforms served merely to perpetuate the institution of serfdom, and to pull one of Russia's Gordian knots even tighter.

In Europe, private property rights for the gentry had taken root and grown to maturity over centuries; in Russia, these rights were a forced growth, a graft that had neither the traditional historical legitimacy of long-time feudal relations nor any stable legal guarantees. The equilibrium of old, pre-Petrine property relations had been destroyed. That is, heretofore the nobles had held land on condition of service to the state. But now, if the nobles were no longer obliged to serve, were the peasants not also freed from any obligation to serve *them?* In the popular mind, the nobles' claim to the land was no more justified than was the peasants'. The iron logic of custom and tradition was impossible to shake. The battle over land rights became a constant threat to stability and a brake on economic development.

The *pomestye* system was never seen as entirely legitimate. This attitude crossed all class lines, as the "lord-and-peasant" mentality of Lev Tolstoy's work so brilliantly demonstrates. Moreover, it is safe to say that up until the twentieth century, owning land and owning property in general were usually seen as one and the same thing. *The absence of any tradition of legitimate ownership is precisely what set Russia so tragically apart from the rest of Europe. That is, she lacked the very psychological and cultural pivot on which all of European capitalism turned.* And therefore it was natural that the "new European rationalism"—all those hastily translated theories refuting the legitimacy of private property— was received with open arms in Russia.

Catherine II, who knew and understood Europe very well, who did a great deal to bring market institutions to Russia (from the simple abolition of internal customs fees to implementation of policies and incentives supporting free industry), also understood how archaic serfdom was and what a historical dead end it represented. One has only to reread her famous *Instruction* to see this. Yet she and her successors, by granting the gentry a clear and absolute right to both lands and the peasants on them and thus launching the gentry as a free estate, were eventually to find themselves at this very dead end.[11]

To free peasants without the land they considered theirs by right would merely exacerbate class conflict and rural poverty; moreover, there was no way to predict how this would affect state revenues. But to free peasants *with* land—which meant taking it away from the gentry— would violate newly won gentry rights. It would be an exercise in absolute rule. The very first right that this new estate had fought for was the right to own its own lands. And the crown feared a palace coup as much as it feared any peasant uprising. The memory of Peter III and Pavel I was all too fresh.[12]

The various agrarian reform projects undertaken in the early nineteenth century, the various polemics surrounding them, and the various secret committees convened during the reigns of Aleksandr I (1801–25) and Nikolai I (1825–55) were all attempts to solve this problem.

One legend, never substantiated but never disproved, claims that when Nikolai I was on his deathbed, he made his successor Aleksandr II swear an oath to cut the knot once and for all—to emancipate the serfs. Whether there is any historical truth to this or not, the idea itself is not so farfetched. The humiliating debacle of the Crimean War had laid bare the gap between Russia and the rest of Europe, and had shown the futility of catch-up attempts made in previous decades and the urgent need to adopt the substance and spirit of European institutions rather than their mere outward form.

3

After the Crimean War, it became clear to most of the Russian political elite that the time had come to rethink national interests, to build new plans, to undertake a new round of reforms that would lay the groundwork for capitalist development. The next sixty years, which saw the abolition of serfdom, judicial and military reforms, the creation of a local governing system *(zemstva),* and the bolstering of property rights, were to bring Russian social institutions closer than ever to European ones and clear the way for rapid industrialization and successful economic development. During this period, one key question emerged: to what extent should Russian capitalism and Russian markets be freed from state controls—first and foremost, in the economically crucial areas of agriculture and landownership?

The legacy of serfdom was a social climate, a social backdrop that would not soon disappear. Decades after the emancipation, it was still a palpable force in Russia's political, economic, and everyday life. Even today, if we look at the results of the 1993 elections region by region, we find that support for market reforms corresponds surprisingly closely to the geographical distribution of the "black-plow" peasants.[13]

Emancipation itself had forced a compromise that left both sides in the age-old dispute over land dissatisfied. As often happens, a reform of this scale gave rise to all sorts of hopes and expectations that could not possibly be fulfilled. Both the peasants and the gentry were unhappy with the results. The former were convinced they had been given too little, the latter were convinced they had lost too much. Some of the lands forcibly alienated from the gentry and granted to the peasants came with conditions; that is, only after peasants had completely paid off the debt did the land become their property free and clear. The commune and its system of *krugovaya poruka* were retained as a mechanism to regulate both taxes paid to the state and compensation paid to former landlords. Moreover, it was the commune, not the individual, to whom lands were granted. In fact, peasants' rights were curtailed, because without permission of the commune they could not get an internal passport or leave the land to find work in the city. If they did so on their own, they could always be summoned back, or even forcibly brought back by the police. Private exchanges of land within the commune were strictly limited, as was the right to leave it. In documents deeding land to peasants, neither location nor boundaries were described with any precision. So the householder, now technically free, was less a property owner than a civil servant working under state supervision. A wave of egalitarian and antiproperty sentiment spread throughout the populace and, as years passed, would give no sign of abating.

It is no surprise that while these long awaited freedoms and incentives sparked industrial development in the cities, they produced the opposite effect in rural areas, which went on to suffer decades of alternating crisis and stagnation. Lack of incentive to increase productivity or to innovate was compounded by a heavy tax burden, by communal taxation, by a growing rural population and artificial restrictions on travel and job mobility. Meanwhile, land itself was in increasingly short supply, and demands for its redistribution became ever more insistent.

The peasants, most of whom had never really accepted Peter and Catherine's agrarian revolutions, still staunchly believed that the land belonged to the tsar, and that the tsar could and should divide it up in such a way that "everyone has enough." Talk of some foreign notion of "private property" did little to change anyone's mind.

The state reacted to this with ever-growing concern, as it strove to expand government control and regulation of agriculture in the late nineteenth-century. This was especially evident during the reign of Aleksandr III, as limitations on peasants' (putative future landowners') rights—restrictions that the liberal authors of the emancipation manifesto had intended to be strictly temporary—were being reinforced and perpetuated for decades to come.

A law passed in 1886 made the division of property among members of a single peasant household far more complicated and difficult than ever before. Another law, promulgated on 8 July 1893, required that lands held by the commune be redistributed at least once every twelve years, and a law issued on 14 December of the same year drastically complicated the process of selling one's holding, even to another commune member. This made leaving the commune virtually impossible.

But the more the state tried to regulate land use and limit the development of private property relations, the deeper the crisis in agriculture, the greater the dissatisfaction and anger of the peasants became. Calls to redraw the property lines became ever more insistent. So by the turn of the century, the war over agricultural policy had escalated drastically. Here the battle lines were clearly drawn: Plehve was on one side; Witte and Stolypin were on the other.[14]

Plehve's credo was quite simple: "Land holdings, inasmuch as they are a matter of national interest . . . cannot be the object of free commerce and exchange, and thus are not subject to ordinary civil law." Hence Plehve's policy included total state control of real property, patriarchal "care and guardianship" of peasants, severe limitations on how much land a single peasant household could own, and efforts to prevent the rise of an independent peasant class (kulaks).[15]

Witte's stance was the polar opposite of Plehve's. He believed that such attempts to perpetuate state control over the peasantry were the main cause of Russia's economic backwardness, that they put the nation at both social and political risk. He saw a clear link between the impossibility of private ownership and the possibility of revolution. Hence the key elements of his program were bringing the civil rights of the peasants into line with the civil rights of other estates; abolishing punitive legal measures applied exclusively to peasants; making peasant communes subject to overall civil law on property ownership; restoring the right to leave the commune; reinforcing rights concerning individual holdings; redefining "household" property as private property belonging to individual household members; and abolishing restrictions on freedom of movement and place of residence.

In 1903, Witte managed to push through a ruling on the abolition of krugovaya poruka (the 12 March ukaz). The manifesto of 11 August

1904 abolished corporal punishment for peasants. But it was not until widespread social unrest spilled over into revolt and revolution in 1905 that the tsarist government was truly persuaded that its paternalistic-statist approach was both dangerous and pointless, that it had to pursue Stolypin's agrarian reform program. Witte's obvious dislike of Stolypin clearly testifies to the former's resentment of the failure to implement reforms over which he had labored so long.

Stolypin's credo was this: "Until the labor spent on our land is of the very highest quality, i.e., until this labor is free rather than forced, our land will be unable to compete with our neighbors'. . . . State paternalism, special considerations and exclusive rights for peasants will merely render them chronically helpless and weak."[16]

Stolypin's agrarian policies show him to be that rare example of a Russian statesmen who actually attempted to limit the state's role in the nation's economy. His decrees of 5 October 1906 and 9 November 1906 gave the peasantry the same status as other estates, guaranteeing their right to divide property within the family; to sell off their holdings, to leave the commune, to convert their share of "the commons" to privately held property, to combine land parcels; and to convert "household property" into individual property. Thus a crucial obstacle to rural development was removed.

The number of peasant households leaving communes in 1906 and 1907 was tiny, but over the next two years grew by leaps and bounds. By 1909, it had peaked at 579,000. One powerful incentive for peasants to leave were the interest payments on land mortgaged to the Peasant Bank. The number of organizations offering mortgages grew and grew; thirty-six municipal and guberniya credit unions were established and a true market in land began to take shape. The volume of land sales in European Russia rose from 157,000 desyatinas in 1908 to 724,000 desyatinas in 1913.

Russia's agricultural sector responded to these new stimuli by growing in both volume and efficiency. The gross national agricultural product of European Russia between 1909 and 1913 was 30 percent higher than it had been in 1900; grain production between 1900 and 1913 increased by 150 percent. Wheat exports nearly doubled.[17]

Russian agriculture never developed so far and so fast as in this short interval between the commune and the collective farm. Its development serves to refute popular notions of the Russian peasantry's "inborn spirit of collectivism" and its "utter antipathy" to the idea of private ownership. Historical experience has shown that neither cliché describes most Russian peasants of the time. I believe that if we manage to create a true agricultural market—especially a market in land—we will see equally striking results, despite the damage that decades of collectivization have done to the Russian work ethic.

Still, the emancipation of 1861 did not bring sudden industrial progress. One major obstacle was the chronic lack of individual savings. A peasantry already overburdened by taxes, by compensation paid to individual landlords, a peasantry deprived (thanks to the perpetuation of the communal taxation system) of any incentive to produce more or work better, could hardly put much into voluntary savings. Nor was the aristocracy, given its long-standing tradition of conspicuous consumption, a reliable source of revenue. The Russian budget ran on a chronic deficit, which sapped faith in the national currency. The private fortunes accumulated by Russian entrepreneurs were hardly enough to transform the country into a new economic dynamo.

There were virtually no institutions capable of encouraging either the saving or the distribution of wealth. Business ethics as such did not exist, and Russia's long-standing tradition of false bankruptcy left little hope that her bank sector could support industrialization over the long term. So, in the 1880s, given the complicated task of catching up without the capital to do so, Russia built its policy around stabilization of state finances and monetary flow.

The fiscal reforms and the tighter tax policy undertaken by Ivan Vyshnegradsky and Sergei Witte managed to guarantee a stable budget surplus of around 20 percent, which laid the groundwork for monetary reform and the restoration of the gold standard.[18] Russia was becoming a highly desirable customer in the global capital market. The nation seemed to be heading toward state-supported capitalist industrialization aimed at replacing imported products with domestic ones. Given the size of the Russian market and Russia's own wealth of resources, there was ample reason to believe that this policy would lead to real progress.

Railroad construction, financed by either direct loans or other forms of state support, was booming. Major capital investments in railroads created a huge market for industrial products, and thus led to the development of a number of interrelated industries. By 1898, the now long-standing stability of state finances ensured Russia's return to the gold standard, and foreign investors were expressing considerable interest in the Russian market. By 1900, these investors were providing 28.5 percent of Russian companies' capital; by 1913 that percentage had risen to 33 percent. A protectionist tariff adopted in 1891 and preferential treatment of domestic Russian suppliers meant that resources funneled into railroad construction also sparked rapid growth in domestic manufacturing. There was a drastic increase in demand for metal, rolling stock, and for contractors. In the 1890s industrial production more than doubled; miles of track had grown by 150 percent.

Yes, the state indeed played a large part in industrial development. Such was the structure of the Russian economy at the time. But more important here is the *direction* of that development. Government's role in running the economy was actually shrinking, thanks to government efforts. Meanwhile the nongovernment sector was growing much more rapidly, becoming the more dominant of the two.

If we look at the tax system of the time, the chief sources of state revenue are fairly obvious. First and foremost was taxation of peasant households: one tax on liquor, another on salt, on matches, on kerosene, et cetera. Russian trade policy, based on massive grain exports and underconsumption at home, clearly reflected the link between capital investment and taxation of the peasantry. As Vyshnegradsky put it, "We may starve, but we will ship."

Meanwhile, turn-of-the-century agricultural production, with limited incentives and limited opportunities for private capital development, had come to a standstill. Despite rapid growth in manufacturing and industry, Russian per capita income still lagged far behind that of Western nations.[19]

The sociopolitical risks of such a policy are obvious. Who knew how much longer the peasants would remain passive, how much heavier a load rural Russia, still burdened by the legacy of serfdom, would be able to bear? Moreover, the very problems involved in financing indus-

trialization encouraged the state to continue to rely on the peasant commune as a fiscal mechanism, which only made a bad situation worse,
and left Russia as backward as ever.

At the turn of the century, no one could really say for certain which
would happen first—a surge in industrial development and the creation
of a domestic manufacturing base that would both free the peasantry
of its huge tax burden and lay a new, more stable financial foundation
for Russian industrialization, or a political crisis that would shatter any
hope of ongoing, stable development. Capitalist industrialization was
in a race against political collapse.

Meanwhile, the corrupt and archaic tsarist regime, paralyzed by the
specter of some vague but inevitable revolution, was clearly doomed.
By the turn of the century everyone knew that, and the only question
was what form the revolution would take. Would the country's economy have time to get on its feet, to ward off the coming blow? Would
the notion of private ownership sink deeply enough into the national
consciousness to prevent this revolution from becoming a programmatic
socialist "eradication of private property"?

Still, while the rapidly escalating conflicts of the first years of the
twentieth century might have slowed the pace of economic development, Russia's chances of winning the race actually improved considerably after the failed revolution of 1905–7. The peasant riots of those
years knocked any remaining illusions about the native humility and
eternal devotion of Russian peasants right out of aristocratic heads.

The sound fiscal foundation laid in the 1890s had allowed Russia to
survive both the Russo-Japanese War and the 1905 Revolution without
major financial upheavals, and to maintain the country's reputation as
a reliable borrower in the years following.

The economic upturn of 1909–13 was clearly different in character, however. The state's role in supporting capital accumulation and
stimulating industrial growth shrank, while savings grew rapidly, and
the volume of private capital mobilized by joint-stock companies also
increased. Domestic bank resources grew, the reputation of private
banks themselves improved, and the latter began to play a more active
role in financing long-term investment projects. The Stolypin reforms

finally cleared the way for boosting agricultural productivity; their positive influence was obvious in the expanding volume of grain exports.

In all of Russian history, this was perhaps the very first economic upsurge set in motion by forces deep within society rather than by the state flat. Russian society was proving itself to he a healthy, self-sustaining system of its own.

Of course, all the old sources of sociopolitical instability remained. The old argument over land and who should be its master dragged on. There was enormous differentiation in income. A rigid, suicidally stubborn bureaucracy, unwilling to make any concessions, was deepening an already deep political rift. It seemed to be going out of its way to provoke an explosion of popular discontent. A new, painfully raw urban proletariat that had lost its allegiance to village traditions but had yet to adapt to city life was a perfect target for socialist agitation. Still—there was hope that steady, sustainable economic growth based on voluntary savings and private investment could create a foundation for a gradual, peaceful resolution of social conflicts.

So it seemed that Russia had managed to lay the groundwork for development, that it might win its race against time. Then came the First World War, and Russia's involvement in it, and Russia's hopes for the future were dashed.

3 The Three Sources and Three Components of Bolshevism[1]

A dark whirlwind of modern ideology
descended upon us from the West . . . .
—Aleksandr Solzhenitsyn

So at the meeting I say what do you mean International? I say what
we've got here is a revolution, a real people's revolt, that's what we've
got. Like with Stepan Timofeevich. Then they ask me well what
about Karla Marksov and I say he's a German, that means he's got to
be a fool But what about Lenin they say. And I say well Lenin, he's
our man, he's peasant, he's Bolshevik, so what that means is all you
out there is Communists.
—Boris Pilnyak, *The Naked Year*

"Turn this imperialist war into a civil war" must be the proletariat's
watchword, its only watchword.
—Vladimir Lenin

I

BOLSHEVISM BECAME A SERIOUS HISTORICAL PHENOMENON ON 28 June 1914, when in the city of Sarajevo a man named Gavrilo Princip (who was no Bolshevik at all, who in fact belonged to nationalist group called Mlada Bosna) assassinated the Archduke Ferdinand, and set off a world war. Aleksandr Potresov, Lenin's coeditor at *Iskra*, rightly noted that Bolshevism took fire not so much from this small spark as from the great conflagration that followed. Potresov considered the "great, crashing wave of Communism" a direct result of the swell created by the First World War. As Yevgeny Shvarts expressed it:

DRAGON: Do you know the day I first appeared on this earth?

LANCELOT: I know that it was a bad day.

DRAGON: It was a terrible day, a day of battle, the day that Attila himself went down in defeat—you know how many warriors had to fall for that. . . . The earth was soaked with their blood. By midnight the leaves on the trees had turned brown. By dawn huge black mushrooms had sprouted under those trees. I followed them. . . . I crawled up after them, from the depths of the earth. I am the son of war. I am war.[2]

Bolshevism was the child of war, and carried the seeds of war within it. Communism was never anything but "War Communism." It was just that as time went on, war simply took on different forms: war among ourselves (civil war), war against the peasants (collectivization), psychological warfare (the Cold War). When Bolshevism eventually lost all these wars, it perished. But as Bertolt Brecht wrote, "the womb that carried the viper can still bear fruit."

The First World War "Bolshevised" Russian society—first and foremost psychologically. I hardly need to remind anyone of the qualitative change in the nature of social tensions during those years of exhausting, seemingly endless trench warfare in which national goals (loyalty to our allies? annexation of Constantinople and the strait? turning back German aggression? aiding our brothers the Serbs?) seemed increasingly incomprehensible to the average Russian, in spite of all the newspaper appeals to patriotism and calls for national defense.

This change in social life and social consciousness can be summarized in a single popular and terrible phrase of the day: "These days gold's worth less than salt; life's somewhere in the middle."

But "blood's a special kind of juice." The shedding of blood is either a criminal act or a holy act. That is, there is no middle ground. Politics may be wrongheaded, they may be compromised. But war (by which

I mean true all-out war, war that requires total exhaustion of a nation's resources) is not Clausewitz's "continuation of politics by other means." It is the annihilation of politics. When war is seen as holy, the state is immensely strengthened; when war is considered criminal, the state perishes.

But in the latter case the state is not the only thing that perishes. All social support structures once considered legitimate also collapse. How wars blast apart the moral framework of a society, how soldiers, believing themselves betrayed, turn into killers, is clearly illustrated in Mikhail Sholokhov's novel *The Quiet Don,* where the hero says, "There is no God. He doesn't exist! If he did, he wouldn't let this happen to his people. Here on the front we've written him off. . . . we've left him to the old folks."[3]

And clearly, the frontline soldiers who'd written off God, who'd come to despise the tsar (as by now did all of Russia, talking of "Tsar Rasputin"), no longer believed in either a nation or a fatherland. The troops who had once been the state's chief line of defense were now its chief and quite heavily armed enemy. Leninist slogans were already firmly fixed in solders' hearts and minds; the air of the front was thick with them. The only thing lacking was a leader who would dare utter these words openly, make them legitimate, pull the pin on this verbal grenade and toss it into the powder keg of an ongoing war. Whoever went furthest in repudiating all existing social and political institutions, whoever shouted loudest that "everything is allowed," whoever was ready to kick open the door, was already assured the victory.

Stripped of their Marxist aura, judged simply in terms of common sense and morality, Lenin's slogans might have looked like nothing more than calls to murder ("turn the imperialist war into a civil war") and robbery ("steal back what was stolen from you"). But with a *theory* to justify and support such actions, everything changed. With such justification and such support, Lenin—the zealot, the fanatic, the born dictator—could indeed turn the whole world upside down.

The First World War created the perfect climate for revolution. Objectively, the situation was extremely grave. Subjectively, it was explosive. Both conscious and subconscious forms of legitimacy that might have ameliorated social tensions were being obliterated; the entire structure of society itself was now seen as illegitimate, and people were now either psychologically prepared to destroy it ("the lower classes won't live like this anymore!") or incapable of defending it ("the upper classes can't live like this anymore!").

One goal and one motto unified everyone. "Stop the war!" (That is, Lenin could hardly rouse the masses by urging them to turn the imperialist war into a civil war—that speech was for the faithful.) The masses had to believe that they could steal back what was rightfully theirs *without* going to war.

And so three very different waves merged to create a sort of super-resonance: the general savagery of wartime, the *Pugachevshchina* of the masses, Leninist-Marxist fanaticism.[4] These were the three sources of Bolshevism. When they finally converged, they set off the greatest explosion in the history of Russia—perhaps in the history of the world.[5]

2

The war also provided Lenin with an almost perfect economic model: a military-industrial complex and military-industrial capitalism. As far as he was concerned, the two were essentially the same thing. Thus militarization of the economy plus monopolization of the economy was the foundation on which Bolshevik experiments with the Russian economy would be based.

Government intervention in manufacturing and distribution had increased sharply once war was declared. Strict government regulation met mobilization needs far better than did a free market. At least so it seemed in both Germany and Russia (although the economic victory eventually went to America, where there was far less government control than in Germany). In Russia, a multitude of military-industrial committees sprang up—"special commissions" on fuel, transport, supply. (Another irony of history is that had it not been for the war and the consequent militarization of the Russian economy, had it not been for those special commissions, Stalin's own "special commissions" might have never existed.)[6]

War might be defined as the greatest possible degree of state interference in the lives of individuals and the life of the society itself—not only on the front lines, but on the home front too. In wartime the state intervenes everywhere, but first of all it intervenes in the economy.

Granted, Marxist doctrine lay at the heart of one of Lenin's best works, *Imperialism, the Highest Stage of Capitalism,* written during the war years. But so did practical experience and a careful analysis of military and industrial interests. In this work Lenin described the military-industrial complex (the model for which was the German wartime economy) and delineated its chief characteristics. As soon as free market capitalism is subjected to rigid state controls, it becomes imperialism. Let me remind the reader of the classic features of imperialism as Lenin defines them: "Imperialism is a separate and distinct stage of capitalism. Three features make it so: imperialism is (1) monopoly capitalism; (2) parasitic or rotting capitalism; (3) dying capitalism."[7]

The economic system that Lenin describes so precisely here is the very one that he consciously and deliberately constructed in Russia, except that in Russia it was called "socialism." In listing these features, he quite correctly focused on a single system-defining principle—the monopolistic nature of an economy that kills off competition and markets. Hence the parasitic nature of such a system, which feeds on both natural resources and "labor resources"; hence the lack of any incentive to grow, to sustain itself, to develop; hence its eventual "stagnation" and "death."

As Lenin well knew, the ultimate form of monopoly is state monopoly. Commenting on protectionism and Russian enterprise, he wrote: "[O]ur industrial satraps [an interesting verbal association with the 'Asiatic mode of production'—Ye. G.] are not representatives of free capital, of strong capital; they are a gang of monopolists that feed on government aid. . . . [T]heir oppression condemns 5/6ths of the population to abject poverty, and the country as a whole to stagnation and rot."[8]

Lenin's goal was to take this system to its logical end. Imperialism would not be total and complete until it was completely merged with the state (i.e., until it was no longer based on independent private ownership).

We all know that Lenin regarded state capitalism (equals imperialism) as a transitional stage, the pupa out of which the butterfly of socialism would eventually emerge. He wrote clearly, unequivocally that:

> [S]tate-monopoly capitalism is the material/financial groundwork of socialism; it is the threshold, the last step on the historical ladder before the step we call "socialism" . . . and there are no steps in between. What must we do to make the "leap" directly from imperialism to socialism? One thing and one thing only: seize power! . . . Our society has matured, it is ripe for the transition to socialism; the war itself has demonstrated this, as it became necessary [for the state—Ye. G.] to concentrate all the nation's resources, to put half a million people into harness and direct them from one *single* center. If this is possible under the leadership of a bunch of petty aristocrats who serve a handful of financial magnates, it is equally as possible under the leadership of politically conscious workers who serve the interests of that 9/10ths of a population exhausted by hunger and war.[9]

And so the chain of logic was forged. Capitalism—state regulation—state-monopoly capitalism (imperialist, decaying, parasitic)—socialism.

3

Lenin also provided a precise formula for the transition from imperialism to socialism. The ruling elite is replaced, a dictatorship is established, and all democratic "superstitions" are done away with. Power is wrested from "petty aristocrats and Junker-boys" and transferred to "politically conscious members of the working class"—that is, Communists. (For some reason, though, at this very moment the barren earth begins to bear fruit: suddenly this new state monopoly ceases to be parasitic, stops rotting, stops dying, and instead "lets a hundred flowers bloom," as the Chinese Marxists used to say.)

Again, Lenin gave us the formula: Communism is imperialism plus the dictatorship of the Communist Party. There is a certain logical final-ity to this. The two sides of the coin complement one another: economic dictatorship/political dictatorship. A totalitarian model in the making. In Russia this formula, unlike the baby talk about Soviet rule and electrification, was applied absolutely and ruthlessly.[10]

I would like to emphasize once more—lest this sound like just another fashionable demonization of Lenin—that his economic plan was by no means some "Satanic plot" aimed at destroying Russia herself. Nor was it a doctrinaire attempt to create a Marxist Utopia, for the simple reason that Marx never proposed anything of the sort. Lenin's platform arose out of real life, out of the practical problems involved in running a militarized economy. It was a hymn to regulation, an apotheosis of centralized control. And while many people at the time took a less radical stance than he did, most of them agreed with him in principle. He was not lying when he wrote:

> You may be assured that you will not find a single speech, a single article in any newspaper, a single resolution by any assembly or official body that does not clearly and definitively acknowledge that only one thing can avert mass starvation and overall disaster. That one thing is the establishment of control, supervision, and regulation by the state: it is the proper distribution of human resources throughout industry, the proper distribution of foodstuffs throughout the populace; it is the husbanding of the people's resources, the elimination of any wasteful use of those resources, it is the conservation of those resources. Control, supervision, accountability—this is our first priority in combatting famine and overall disaster.[11]

This sounds more like the September 1994 issue of *Pravda* than one from September 1917! Indeed, those who for the past four years have been gleefully predicting "disaster and famine" offer the same formula for averting "imminent disaster" as Lenin did—that is, government regulation. The only difference is that today these words tend to stick in the craw, because over the last seventy years we have watched just how well state controls have "husbanded the people's resources" and "eliminated any wasteful use."

Remarkable, too, are the specific measures Lenin advocates for establishing state controls, which, as he correctly puts it, were acknowledged under the tsarist regime:

1. Consolidation of all banks into a single central bank, the operations of which will be regulated by the state, or [in other words] nationalization of all bank operations.
2. Nationalization of syndicates, i.e., the largest manufacturing and processing monopolies (sugar, oil, coal, metallurgy etc.).
3. Abolition of trade secrets as such . . .[12]

To what existing system do Lenin's *Imperialist Notebooks* relate? We have already mentioned his most immediate source of inspiration— the German military-industrial complex. Other sources, more general in nature, were the various trusts, concerns, and cartels that had proliferated at the turn of the century, especially in the USA. Unlike the military-industrial complex, which was clearly a temporary phenomenon, a mobilized, forced effort, these trusts and cartels were a natural outgrowth of capitalism, its next logical stage. And if indeed they were its most advanced stage, as Lenin claimed, they would also be its last.

Many people agreed. Studies of imperialism were very fashionable in those days, and Lenin's study owes much to the works of Kautsky and Hilferding, even as it challenges them. It might be considered a "scholarly commentary" to Jack London's *The Iron Heel*, which describes the United States moving from free-market capitalism to state-monopoly imperialism and finally to political dictatorship.[13]

But at one point, precisely because monopoly capitalism, even in embryonic form, was a threat and a danger to free enterprise and political democracy, precisely because it was so obviously leading to a dead end rather than open-ended development, because it was so obviously a cancer on the body of capitalism, American society set out to do battle against it. At the turn of the century Congress and the president adopted a number of antitrust measures meant to "cut off the air supply" to monopolies, to break their stranglehold on the market. Here Lenin was absolutely on the mark, in that only a political dictatorship can impose and support total monopolization of a national economy.

Only in alliance with the state (a dictatorial state, of course) can monopoly capitalism win out over free-market competition, crush it, and thus become a finished and complete system. This, Lenin writes, is where the "enormous power of capitalism and the enormous power of the state come together as a single machine."[14]

Just as free and open competition in politics (democracy, in other words) is tied to free and open competition in the market, so are economic monopolies bound to political monopolies (dictatorships). But oddly enough, if it is the Communist Party, the Communist oligarchy, that holds the monopoly, the system automatically becomes progressive, historically justified, and justifiably Communist! For "socialism is simply a state-capitalist monopoly created to promote the general welfare of the people." Lenin wrote: "Pure imperialism, [i.e.] imperialism without a capitalist base, has never existed, does not exist, and never will."[15]

This "capitalist base" is the marketplace; it is private ownership of property. Lenin was right about this: as long as monopolies are cooking along with everything else in the common capitalist pot, we cannot talk about purely "imperialistic," "monopolistic," or "parasitic" capitalism.

Since his day, the West has experienced not revolution but "Keynesian" evolution. States have intervened in economics much more actively than in the past, and many Western countries have nationalized entire sectors of the economy. Gigantic transnational megacorporations have taken shape. As a rule, they do not belong to anyone personally; there is no single "boss." These are joint-stock corporations where no one (except perhaps some other faceless corporate giant) holds a majority of shares. Actually, they are more like ministries than companies (although these companies' financial and technological capacity is far greater than that of the average Russian ministry).

It might seem that what we have here are the same old bureaucratic behemoths who plan years in advance, whose countless executives and managers are utterly alienated from real life and real business, who mainly profit from accepting bribes and sabotaging change—in other words, organizations totally analogous to our old Soviet ministries (Leninist monopolies). To some extent they are just that. As early as the 1930s even Harold L. Ickes, then U.S. Secretary of the Interior, was declaring that big business was a bureaucracy.

So has the West, being subject to these same laws of economics and history, inevitably come around to state capitalism, to its own "Western" version of socialism? This is precisely what many people in the 1960s understood the popular term "convergence" to mean. Long before that, in the very early years of the twentieth century, Karl Kautsky had predicted this very march toward socialism as part of his theory of "ultraimperialism."

However, state capitalism in the Leninist sense has never really taken shape in the West. The reason lies in the market economy and the market rules by which even major corporations must play.

As a result, these huge concerns are open to technological advances, and they function much more efficiently than do their state-owned counterparts (not to speak of state-socialist ministries), although they are perhaps less efficient than many smaller firms.

4

State-oligarchy capitalism (= imperialism = socialism) in the Leninist sense resembles Marx's "Asiatic mode of production" more than it does anything else. Paradoxical as this might seem, Lenin's seemingly "ultrawestern" socioeconomic system in fact dovetails with Eastern tradition. One essential feature is common to both: political authority and property ownership are one; property ownership is a function of political authority. Imperialism à la Lenin was not the final step, the highest stage in the development of a capitalist socioeconomic system. It was quite the opposite. It was, in fact, a reduction of that system to institutions and structures the West had abandoned hundreds of years before (although the system's reliance on twentieth-century technology was never reduced). Many people understood this perfectly well even as the Soviet era began to dawn.

Half of the intelligentsia, looking for explanations and analogies, saw the October Revolution as a radical, Western, bourgeois internationalist phenomenon. The other half, however, came much closer to the truth: it focused on the profoundly reactionary, "imperial," "Eastern," "populist-anarchist" nature of the revolt.

Hence Plekhanov asserted that the Bolshevik's nationalization of land would lead to the establishment of "the same economic order that had been the foundation of all the great despotic regimes of the East," calling Bolshevism "something out of China," an "antirevolutionary" and "reactionary" step backwards for Russian history.

One of Russia's most perceptive and philosophically minded poets, Mikhail Voloshin, defined the essence of the Revolution in this way:

> Blow, blow, wintry element,
> Drift over ancient graves:
> This wind bears Russia's fate,
> Russia's mad and awful fate,
> This wind bears all the lead of years, of Rus'
> And its Malyutas, its Ivans and Godunovs
> its predators, oprichniki and streltsy,
> its butchers and its skinners,
> old dreams of tsars, the waking life of Bolsheviks.
> What here has changed? The symbols and the sovereigns?
> The same storm rages over all the roads:
> The madness of the tsars is in the commissars
> The madness of revolt is in the tsars . . . .
>
> Flung forward over centuries
> Against all natural law . . . .
>
> Be it now or then, it's all the same
> Wolf teeth, wolf grin,
> Stale air and feral mind,
> The searching and the scheming
> Of Secret Chancelleries,
> The drunken whoop of animals possessed,
> The whistle and the burn of whip and lash,
> The savage dream of military posts,
> Phalansteries, parades and drills
> Of Pavels, Peters, Arachkeevs,
> Grim dreams of Gatchina, of fearsome Petersburg,
> The designs of brutal surgeons,
> The headsman's reach and swing. . . . [16]

In this synthesis of the dictatorship of the party and a state-monopoly (imperialistic) economy Voloshin saw the most frightening variation that Russian historical evolution could produce: tsarist, autocratic social-ism. This is precisely how Saltykov-Shchedrin's *History of a Town* ends: the ultimate nightmare of "autocratic communism" in the person of Ugrium-Burcheev.[17]

This is the socialism that conservative Konstantin Leontiev called down on Russia with a sort of grim delight, "to freeze [her], lest she rot." He wrote point-blank that for Russia:

> socialism is the feudalism of the future . . . as radical revolution turns into entrenchment, coercion, becomes discipline, even slavery. . . . I have a sense, a premonition, that our Most Holy Slavic Orthodox Tsar will yet one day take the socialist move-ment in hand . . . and, with the blessing of the Church, set the socialist way of life in the place of the bourgeois-liberal one. And this new socialism will serve three masters: the commune, the Church and the Tsar.[18]

One has to admit that Leontiev's prediction of a "new Middle Ages" comes close to historical truth, especially as concerns socialist servi-tude, communes and collective farms, and the annihilation of the bour-geois-liberal way of life. His intuition did not fail him; he knew the demons of Russian history all too well.

The October Revolution washed away Russia's thin layer of Western culture with blood, scraped it away with bayonets. What then rose to the top were the ancient and powerful strata of "marginals" from both city and countryside. This was, as S. L. Frank put it, an invasion of home-grown barbarians. The new elite was made up of the "wild folk," char-acters out of Zoshchenko and Platonov.[19] Essentially medieval modes of autocratic rule returned to work in concert with modern technol-ogy and bureaucratic institutions. (Small wonder that Berdiaev titled his 1924 book *The New Middle Ages*.) Even some Communists, in their occasional moments of clarity, realized this (Stalin was described as "Genghis Khan with a telephone"). The Bolshevik government's jour-ney from St. Petersburg to Moscow in 1918 was rife with symbolic mean-ing: it was a return from Europe, from "Petersburg Russia," to the medieval kingdom-khanate of Muscovy. (In 1919 the territory controlled by the Bolsheviks was almost exactly the same as that once ruled by the Grand Princes of Muscovy.) The locomotive of Russian history was hurtling eastward. Any "Western influence" was by this time purely superficial.

All this suggests that Lenin's so-called socialism was something that ran deep in the grain of Russia's own history, that it was organic to this kingdom of "Malyutas, Ivans and Godunovs," the empire of "Pavels, Peters, Arachkeevs." It was merely one of several possible lines of imperial/autocratic development. Of course, what Lenin introduced into the Russian body politic was a virus. But the Russian system was certainly ready to absorb it. However, this was not some awful virus of anarchy and destruction, as most dim-witted civil servants feared at the time. It was a virus that would foster the pathological, malignant growth of the state.

So the choice between a self-sustaining and evolving civil society and a despotic, quasi-Eastern regime was made. Yet Lenin's blueprint for socialism represented something absolutely unique, something that set it quite apart from both Western variations on state capitalism (imperalism) and classic Asiatic modes of production, something that, while it owed much to Russian autocratic-bureaucratic and communal tradition, also rejected much of it.

Only in this fusing of Eastern despotism/dictatorship in politics, state monopoly in economics, and a Communist ideology that rejected the very notion of private property, only in this organic synthesis cemented by blood and fired in the furnaces of civil war, could a truly totalitarian monolith take form.

The fact of the matter is that while "the Asiatic mode of production" had no tradition of respect for private property, no tradition of legitimate private ownership, neither did it have any tradition of rejecting them out of hand. Such rejection was all the more unthinkable under state capitalism. So in no other society have we ever seen this idea of total repudiation of private ownership, a repudiation imposed socially, psychologically, and juridically by the state.

This is what Lenin and the Bolsheviks managed to do. That is, they methodically, viciously, and thoroughly wiped out the very notion of private property. Lenin was working out of clearly doctrinarian, dogmatist motives. But in objective terms, this was the "missing link" (another of his favorite phrases) in the unique chain that led to truly unprecedented, universal dictatorship, the last brick in the building of perfect despotism. This was the root, the core of a new historical order, a Communist totalitarian order. That is why, by the way, the Communist totalitarian order was more perfect than was its Fascist counterpart (which was also a combination of state capitalism and political dictatorship, but with a different state ideology—in this case chauvinism and racism).

Here we see not merely the suppression of private ownership, but its total eradication: complete abolition of any legal standing, total delegitimization in the popular mind. Here we have the foundation for a total, monolithic, political, and economic state dictatorship. This was the watershed between "imperialism" and "socialism," as socialism became the highest (the last) stage of the Asiatic mode of production.

The Asiatic mode of production and its "European projection" (state-monopoly production) presupposed that for the system to be internally perfect and complete, private property had to be completely eliminated; the state had to seize it all. Of course, this also would have been the height of absurdity—crossing the boundaries of human history as we know it (Eastern *or* Western) and going off into some new dimension. But totalitarianism loves those "final solutions" that erase all previous history. German totalitarianism sought a final solution to its "Jewish question"; Russia sought a final solution to its "market question."

Of course, in order to justify such extremes, one needs an ideology powerful enough to clothe absolute expropriation in absolutely beautiful utopian rhetoric. Here socialism fit the ideological bill perfectly. Socialism did not advocate state ownership or "nationalization"; it called for popular ownership, the "socialization" of property, an immediate "humanization" of property relations. Meanwhile, it never actually denied that all property would henceforth belong to the state. In order to make the great leap over that logical chasm, to somehow put an equal sign between the "statization" and the "socialization" of property, some verbal acrobatics were required. And so it was declared that, under the dictatorship of the benevolent Communist Party, the all-powerful state would simply and miraculously "wither away."

Lenin's final solution might look something like this: Socialism = the political dictatorship of the Party + a state-monopoly economy + Communist ideology. However, since we are dealing with a synthesis rather than an arithmetical sum, the parts undergo a certain change as they combine. So we no longer have traditional imperialism (presumably rotting and decaying, but nonetheless a form of state capitalism) that presupposes a market, private ownership, et cetera. No, here we have the emergence of a qualitatively new order, a system in which, *as a matter of principle,* there is no such thing as a market.

4 Property, the Nomenklatura, and Nomenklatura Property

All of Communist theory can be expressed in one single phrase: the abolition of private property!
—Marx and Engels

The bureaucracy has the state in its possession. . . . [I]n essence, the state is the bureaucracy's private property.
—Marx

I

A COMPLETE HISTORY OF THE RELATIONSHIP BETWEEN THE SOVIET nomenklatura and the Soviet nomenklatura state, the history of their torturous conflicts and the eventual alienation of the former from the latter has yet to be written. But for the moment we can posit at least this: the Soviet system was devoured from within, by its own ruling class. Marx wrote that the bourgeoisie was digging its own grave.[1] Well, the Communist oligarchy, too, may have dug its own grave, but this was a shrewd and mercenary gravedigger, and it aimed to profit from its own death. More accurately, it aimed to turn a funeral into a party, a celebration of liberation from the old system and of the birth of a new one—which, by the way, it would also control.

This became obvious between 1989 and 1991. I hardly need mention that the most active part of the liberal-democratic intelligentsia (the "project managers of perestroika") were by no means dissidents;

to the contrary, the majority of them had government ties of one sort or another. This may be almost inevitable when a political revolution is preceded by a spiritual one.

Much more important here is the fact that the rank-and-file nomenklatura, political and economic alike, took "the anticommunist revolution" quite calmly, and in fact was rather sympathetic to it. This explains why this particular revolution was so easy, so bloodless, and yet remained only half-finished, why later so many people felt that their hopes and ideals for social change had been betrayed.

And, of course, the true nature of the nomenklatura-antinomenklatura revolution became clear when the time came to divvy up state property, and everyone saw that the nomenklatura and its "subsidiaries" ("Komsomol Inc.," for example) were the first to get rich. Terms like nomenklatura privatization, nomenklatura capital, nomenklatura capitalism, and nomenklatura democracy became common parlance.

In the Manichaean minds of that part of our society obsessed with conspiracy theories, what we had here was a global conspiracy, instigated by the old Soviet nomenklatura (of course) and its cronies in Washington and Tel Aviv (But look here. . . . This was a planned disaster . . . a wolfish plot backed by trillions of U.S. dollars. . . . These dollars were what launched the entire thing . . .)—a conspiracy that in some paranoid fantasies went as far as "CIA agents in the Politburo."

There is no doubt that what took place in 1990 and 1991 was a major geopolitical upheaval, regardless of one's attitude pro or con. It not only took most Soviet citizens by surprise (dissidents included); it stunned professional Sovietologists too. Look at what noted historians Aleksandr Nekrich and Mikhail Heller were writing at the time: "Now, on the eve of its 70th anniversary, this state born in October of 1917 is rounding out the eighth decade of the twentieth century as the last world empire. From Cuba to Vietnam, from Czechoslovakia to Angola, the sun indeed never sets over the Soviet empire. . . . Its success as a system is obvious."[2] This was the view from a West still panicking at the thought of Communist aggression.

Communism collapsed for any number of reasons. But our focus here is its internal disintegration: the social and psychological degeneration of the elite, and the subsequent "trickle-down" political and economic degeneration of the system itself.

In the very first days of the regime, the Soviet nomenklatura sealed itself off from its own people, not to speak of the rest of the world. After all, it had its own issues to resolve—chief among which was to insure itself against a "capitalist restoration." The only real way to do so was to give ever more power to the "guarantor"—that is, the Communist elite. As it turned out, this very elite would eventually become the "chief restorer" of capitalism in Russia.

The degeneration of the elite, and of the system, is a very long story. What follows is a brief outline.

1917–1921. War Communism. Private ownership is abolished in areas controlled by Communist forces. Civil war, Red Terror. The nomenklatura is locked in a fight to the death; they see themselves as latter-day Jacobins.

1921–1929. NEP. Peacetime, a breather, a mixed economy, the closest thing to an Eastern state (or a "Leninist imperialist" one). Subsistence economies, small businesses, private ownership, state-capitalist enterprises, and socialist ownership exist side by side. Communism's first major crisis, the first hint of "degeneration," of a bourgeois Thermidor.[3] Meanwhile, the new state is dropping the iron curtain, waging an ideological war against the rest of the world (and against "vestigial social elements" at home).

1929–1953. Totalitarianism. The only period in which Communism truly triumphs in Russia. It reaches its peak in 1937, when the nation "ascended from the abstract to the concrete," from theory to real life. It would be more accurate to say that this was a reduction of life to theory. An ideological steamroller flattens the economic landscape. Barring some essential but relatively minor exceptions (a garden plot, a few head of livestock—people have to get by, you know) a truly monolithic system of state ownership takes shape. Private property ceases to exist. It is here the qualitative differences between this new system and the old "Asiatic mode of production" make themselves most obvious. Government policy differs too, as it conducts what is essentially a bloody civil war redefined as "escalation of class conflict."

1953–1985. Descent from the "Communist yawning heights." Another crisis, "second call." While total state ownership still appears to be the norm, certain "shadow" movements begin to stir within it. An exclusively "bureaucratic" market comes into being. Deep within the protective sac of state ownership—or more accurately, "pseudostate" ownership—the embryo of quasi-private or ur-private ownership begins to develop, still hidden from view, but potentially powerful. A barely visible process of "preprivatization" goes hand in hand with the degeneration of the nomenklatura. The social structure again begins to resemble Lenin's imperialism, state capitalism, or even Eastern despotism, but in a some-how distorted form. Outwardly, the political situation is relatively sta-ble: an ongoing Cold War with the outside world and with Russian society. This is a positional war, a static, almost bloodless one.

1985–1991. The end of Communism. The third bell rings, the cur-tain rises; everything that had lain submerged during the previous period now rises to the surface. Nomenklatura privatization begins in earnest and comes into the open; private ownership is legalized; no one even talks about state (i.e., totalitarian) ownership any more. The Soviet nomenklatura becomes a quasi-capitalist elite. By the end of this period, the system no longer looks like classically defined imperialism, let alone Eastern despotism, but rather like some transitional form on its way to becoming "Western," moving toward a market economy, an open society, and free-market capitalism. Granted, these changes are still entirely reversible. In political terms, the state has lost the psycho-logical cold war both at home and abroad and is in full retreat. It will eventually collapse and ultimately disappear.

2

Yet there is a rigid framework of logic underlying all these historical metamorphoses. Real, empirical human history has merely fleshed out this skeleton logic with fact.

Let us recall our two epigraphs for this chapter, Marx's two formulas. Communism abolishes private property. The state is the property of the bureaucracy.

These two maxims are the jaws of a logical vise in which any soci-ety built on Marxist principles is caught. These two formulas are an outline for the shortest of short courses on the history of the CPSU (Bolshevik). Logically, sociologically, psychologically, they are the frame of the grand but doomed house that Lenin built.

We can posit a number of consequences flowing from Marx's assertions: (1) By abolishing private ownership, the Communists turn all property into state property. (2) State property is the collective property of the bureaucracy. (3) Bureaucrats or bureaucratic clans inevitably seek to turn state property into private property (their own).

Expropriation of private property—state/bureaucratic property—private/bureaucratic property; this is the socialist formula, birth to death, cradle to grave.

In principle, what we have here is an individual example of the general problem faced by all Eastern despotic regimes: the universal desire of government officials to "privatize" their power, to turn power into property.

The failure of the system was guaranteed by the inevitability of the transition from stage two to stage three, by the "involuntary reflex" to privatize. This reflex could be controlled only by faith in a sacrosanct ideology that rejected private property out of hand, by fear of violating the postulates of that faith.

Communism, for all its pretensions to scientific and rational thought, was from its very beginnings a spiritual order whose raison d'être went far beyond reason or fact and entered into the realm of pure faith (pure faith and pure fear, that is). Ideology (faith in it, fear of violating it) alone stood between the right to manage and control state property, and the ever-present opportunity to line one's own pockets.

Let us recall the essential components of Bolshevism: dictatorship of the state in economics and politics, dictatorship of the bureaucracy. But if there is no ideological dictate over the bureaucracy itself, the more totalitarian the order becomes, the more powerful the ruling bureaucracy also becomes—and the more swiftly it degenerates, and takes whatever it can get before it dies.

Therefore, keeping the ideology intact kept the system itself intact, and a key component of that ideology was the war against private property. This alone prevented Communist totalitarianism from "reverting" to state capitalism, and the Soviet nomenklatura from becoming "new capitalists." (Obviously, these antiproperty components were absolutely incompatible with other components within the system; this was, after all, an ideology founded on economic determinism and historical materialism, an ideology whose proclaimed purpose was "to satisfy the needs of the working people"—not to attain some vague, immaterial, spiritual goals. Nonetheless, in the 1920s private ownership of the means of production was strictly taboo, and even ownership of personal property by the nomenklatura was strictly regulated, at least officially.)

For ideology to lead to real action, a new generation of people "steel-willed" but "pure in mind and body" had to be forged. But for all the romantic enthusiasm of one era (followed by self-effacing irony of later ones), the USSR never really managed to create, let alone educate or train, anyone remotely like that.

In the 1930s the official propaganda around such efforts was especially ferocious, and it seemed that many people were indeed truly and sincerely trying to recast themselves as what writer Ilya Ehrenburg dubbed "PCPs"—perfect Communist people.[4] But 1930s Moscow was also the setting of Mikhail Bulgakov's novel *Master and Margarita*. At one point Woland asks himself, "Have Muscovites really changed at all?" and then answers his own question.

> Well they . . . well, people are people. They like money, but then again they always have. . . . Humans have always loved it, whatever it was made of . . . leather, paper, brass, gold. . . . Granted, they're fools, they're idiots . . . but so what. . . . surely there's a little goodness and mercy down deep in their hearts. . . . they're your usual people, more or less just like all the ones that came before. . . . it's just the housing problem that has made this bunch so nasty.[5]

Truly, that's how it's always been. But there had never been a political system that so madly denied this "human, all too human" feeling. Never yet had there been a system that considered the desire for money and property a mortal threat.

Woland's question was essentially the same one that Leon Trotsky, the "demon of revolution," asked himself at the end of the civil war. He was horrified by his own answer:

> Once the tension had eased and the nomads of revolution began to adopt a settled way of life [and were dubbed the "nomenklatura"—Ye. G.] . . . all the petit-bourgeois traits, sympathies, and tastes of a smug and self-satisfied bureaucracy began to awaken within them, to come to life, to grow. None of this in itself ran counter to Party principle. But the reigning mood was complacent, self-satisfied, trivial. . . . The Bolshevik was finding the philistine within.[6]

This psychological metamorphosis among the faithful was termed "the degeneration of the Bolsheviks." Yet what this change demonstrated was not degeneration, but human nature at work. These functionaries had no thought of challenging Party principles or the Party line. All they wanted was what, after any coup, any revolution, any victorious (and now ruling) party would want. They wanted something for themselves.

Of course, at the time it was less a matter of "primitive capital accumulation" than of basic survival, of resolving the question of ownership on a purely everyday, consumer level. And again, that resolution would in no way run counter to the Party principles.

At the end of the 1920s the notorious "Party limit" was abolished.[7] By the mid-1930s the difference between the living standard of the nomenklatura and "simple Soviet citizens" had grown as wide as the pre-revolutionary gap between tsarist officialdom and the poorest of the urban poor. After the Second World War, top figures in the military-industrial complex joined the ranks of the traditional elite (high-level Party officials, diplomats, army brass). Top trade and commerce officials had always enjoyed a certain wealth.

However, this ever-expanding range of privileges could not entirely resolve the hungry nomenklatura's "social issues." It was not simply that, as the saying goes, appetite comes with eating, but that the bureaucratic appetite always seemed to exceed the amount of food available in even the best-stocked Party stores. The urge to own "real property" as well as personal property, the need to own land, financial organizations, manufacturing plants, trading and commercial concerns, et cetera, constituted an often unrecognized but nevertheless painful "social complex." And this is where the needs of the nomenklatura began to come into conflict with official Party doctrine. Trotsky rather aptly noted this when he wrote in the 1930s:

> If . . . [the bureaucracy—Ye. G.] now considers it possible to introduce ranks and decorations, then as the next stage, it will seek support for itself in the realm of property. Some might object that a high-ranking official would hardly care what form of property ownership prevailed, as long as it assured him the income he needed. This reasoning ignores not only the fact that a bureaucrat's rights are never entirely stable, but also the question of his progeny and their future. Our new cult of the family has hardly appeared out of the blue. Privilege is not really privilege if one cannot pass it on to one's children. Yet—the right to will property to one's heirs is inseparable from the right to own it. That is, being the director of a concern is not enough; only being a shareholder is. A victory for the bureaucracy in this crucial area would signal its transformation into a new class of "haves."[8]

In this perceptive sociological analysis, Trotsky anticipated Milovan Djilas's theory of a "new class."[9] Of course, Trotsky was all too loyal to Marxist theory in identifying the very existence of a "class" by some relationship to means of production. Yet he does provide a simple and profound explanation of the nomenklatura's desire to own property. The urge to own is part and parcel of the urge to start a family, to reproduce. Trotsky named his book *The Revolution Betrayed*. He might just as well have titled it *The Decline of the State, or the Influence of Family and Property.*

Thus a sentence on the system was already pronounced. "Fish rot from the head down." The more powerful the socialist state becomes (as it moves into "developed socialism") and the more privileged its ruling class, the sooner and surer that class begins to degenerate, to decline, turn bourgeois—first psychologically, then economically. The Soviet nomenklatura began to break out of its socialist framework like a chick pecking out of its shell. This process of breaking out had nothing to do with any "faults" or "deficiencies" or "Stalinist perversions" of a workable system: it had to do with the system itself, which carried the seed of its own swift and inevitable destruction. Unlike many of Trotsky's other prophecies, this one actually came true.

3

The New Economic Policy (NEP) created the first prerequisite for the eventual "degeneration" of a once revolutionary nomenklatura: while maintaining a political dictatorship and a monopoly on government authority (command positions in property use and allocation), the architects of NEP also hastened to form alliances with other powerful economic groups ("Nepmen" and kulaks first of all) and to move toward limited denationalization of property—a course of action, by the way, not unlike the "Chinese way" that our current nomenklatura has been so enthralled with of late.

NEP might have been the 1920s version of a classic Thermidor—a possibility widely discussed in Russian émigré literature at the time. With the "left opposition" in rout, it seemed that the Stalinist leadership had cleared the way for the bureaucratic state to step back from incipient totalitarianism, to embrace "nomenklatura-state capitalism" while still maintaining the dictatorship of the Party and the GPU. The "make yourselves rich" slogans aimed at the peasantry were equally applicable to the nomenklatura.

But as we all know, there was no Thermidor in the 1920s. Instead, Russia took its own "great leap forward," and thanks to the shockworkers of the OGPU and "the rest of the nation" the house of totalitarianism was finally built.

It would be naive to blame all this on Stalin alone. The nomenklatura itself was not ready for a Thermidor. Soviet society was hardly monolithic, and most Bolsheviks were afraid, not without reason, that they would not be able to hold on in the face of massive political and social unrest. The old guard might well retake Russia, and for the commissars this meant not only the loss of property and power, but something even more dangerous. The civil war had kept the Bolshevik nomenklatura on the hook, had bound it by blood and complicity. There was nowhere to retreat. In fact, the Bolsheviks had set themselves up. Even in victory, the position of a Red factory manager, a people's commissar (military or civilian, no matter), a professional Party operative had never been entirely secure. The ruling bureaucracy understood this perfectly well. And fear made them hold fast to the ideology that itself held the system fast. They also still had some reserves of unspent messianic energy, and some element of belief in a socialist, antiproperty Utopia. This complex mix of fear, survival instinct, and faith was what made a Thermidor, a revolution from above, impossible in the Russia of the 1920s.

In fact, the opposite happened. The nomenklatura launched a frontal assault on the entire nation: "Left, left, left!"[10] Any remaining scraps of private property were confiscated; state ownership became absolute; collectivization plowed over and through all of rural Russia. The totalitarian state was now a finished product; the Leninist state became a Stalinist one (1930–53).

Meanwhile bureaucratic privilege grew and expanded. But so did strife within the bureaucracy. As the nomenklatura was tightening its grip on the country, Stalin was tightening his grip on the nomenklatura, generously applying both the carrot of privilege and the stick of repression—a personal version of Trotsky's permanent revolution, an "escalation of the class struggle" that allowed him to bend official necks so far under the Party yoke that most of those necks eventually snapped, leaving no heads to even think about a Thermidor. In those days, if anyone thought about anything at all, they thought about footsteps on the stairs in the middle of the night: "Good lord, they can't be coming for *me*, can they?!" And so Bolshevism itself was indeed frozen "so as not to rot," locked in a state of permanent revolutionary ascension for a good twenty-five years, until May 5, 1953.

4

Over those years, however, a certain internal ideological metamorphosis took place. Many scholars took notice, among them, scholar

N. Ustryalov, who as early as 1920 had asserted that Russian Bolshevism was already changing its colors, that it was turning into something that might be called "national Bolshevism." The term, coined in Germany in 1919 as an analogy to "national socialism," became common parlance in Russia after the publication of a collection of essays called *Smena Vekh*. The meaning is easy enough to decipher if we recall the famous *Vekhi* of 1909. There was never any real polemic between the two collections.[11]

In fact the *smenovekhovtsy* were Bolshevik "fellow travelers." Swept up in the wake of European intellectual currents in the 1920s and 1930s, they were part of the wave that celebrated dynamism and youth and strength, that set Fascism, Nazism, and Bolshevism against "aged and feeble" and "toothless" democracy. As Karel Čapek so aptly noted: "Is there anything [any movement] so destructive / fatal, so awful, so senseless that some intellectual won't take its part, and won't hope, in so doing, to change the world?"[12]

Émigré intellectuals were far ahead of the curve in their early enthusiasm for national Bolshevism. Only recently, in Gennady Zyuganov's "new and improved" version of the Russian Communist Party, have the Communists finally stripped off the "filth of internationalism" and become both true nationalists and true Bolsheviks. Until the end of the hegemonic Soviet empire, the messianic and internationalist ideology was a constant attribute of the state idea.

The *smenovekhovtsy* both escalated and oversimplified the situation. Bolshevik rhetoric, while indulging in the crudest sort of "Black Hundreds" propaganda (especially between 1945 and 1953, and in the 1970s and early 1980s) still tended to pay ritual homage to internationalism. This is still the case: our national-Bolsheviks like to talk about "purely Russian interests," but in the same breath demand the restoration of the old Soviet Union. And certainly, while the "ethnic cleansing" of Moscow's intellectual elite was received with joy by national-Bolsheviks (who to this day idealize Stalin for doing the very same thing), the purge has hardly affected the real essence of the Communist regime—has not altered its radical-statist stance.

The real ideological change that occurred between the 1920s and 1953 was quite a different phenomenon. As time went by, the system had simply run out of ideological energy, lost its attraction. Fearing some new act of revolution, it had mercilessly exorcised the revolutionary spirit that had once informed it—for now such a revolutionary act could only be directed against the victorious system, the Communist state itself.

This in turn led to a fossilization of the ideology. It was reduced to mere ritual, and the most vivid exemplar of this fossilized ritual was Party ideologist Mikhail Suslov, the cruel "guardian of stability" who reigned from 1947 to 1982.

In fact, this loss of substance, this preservation of purely outward, ritual forms, was the first step toward "sobering up" the system. Form without content soon ceases to be perceived as sacred, and becomes merely annoying. Junior officials who came to prominence after the 1937 purges were, as a rule, devoid of the romantic illusions typical of their predecessors. They were standard bureaucrats with standard ambitions for a standard, successful bureaucratic career. They were perfectly willing to conform to the standard rituals of the "Church of Marxism—just as tsarist functionaries had conformed to those of the Russian Orthodox Church. They held no profound convictions. As Ortega y Gasset wryly put it, "Russia is about as Marxist as the Germans of the Holy Roman Empire were Roman."[13] For many of these officials, the instinct to possess, the desire to own, became a real mania. Communism's "Church militant," was becoming the "Church cynical." Ideology was losing its spiritual content, was becoming a hollow shell now filled by hypocrisy and cynicism. "The USSR is a country of lies, of absolute lie, all-encompassing lie," wrote Sovietologist Boris Suvarin in the 1930s. "[T]he USSR is a lie from top to bottom. Four words, four letters, four lies."[14]

The anticorrosive coating of ideology that had protected the nomenklatura from rust and rot was thinning. The faith was gone, the fear remained. Once Stalin was dead, fear too seemed to be on the wane.

5

After "the iron winter" came "the thaw." A totalitarian society was becoming a merely authoritarian one. Naturally, this was a "trickle-down" process, beginning at the top. None of these hard-line, "loyal Stalinist" comrades-in-arms wanted to preserve the system unchanged (no more than did their Politburo counterparts some thirty years later, in the first days of perestroika). But neither did they ever intend to undermine the system itself.

Yet once they had almost instinctively taken the first step on that "slippery slope" of reform, they had, unbeknownst to themselves, marked the beginning of the end of socialism. And this time the clock didn't stop. It kept ticking away until, on 21 August 1991, the third bell rang.

It had taken forty years for this long-needed and so belated Thermidor to arrive, forty years to build up first moral and ideological strength and resources, then social and financial ones.

In the 1950s, once the juggernaut of repression had stopped crushing every living thing in its path, the seeds of a civil society began to sprout and grow. By the 1970s a relatively stable social situation plus improvements in the standard of living (uneven, but real) had led to increasing social differentiation. In the 1930s and 1940s, "camp dust" had blown back and forth between the barracks of the prisoners and the barracks of the guards, over and through the barbed wire nominally separating the two. People were no more than dust in the wind, and this was called "society."[15] Between the 1950s and the 1970s, real social institutions begin to take shape. Of course, this new civil society felt about as comfortable in the belly of the Soviet state as Jonah felt in the belly of the whale. But like Jonah, it survived. It even began to grow.

Communism's monism, its logical integrity, was both its great strength and its greatest and most terrible weakness. Once the system began to collapse, it collapsed systematically, consistently, irreversibly. Once the protective layer of ideology could no longer prevent corrosion, there was no restoring the structure. Corrosion was gnawing it away, and, while the facade, the shell, the external attributes still stood, what they housed was changing every day.

The nomenklatura of the mid-1950s, now free of Stalin but still fearful of the sort of bloodbath out of which it had itself emerged, tried to ensure against the possibility of another round of "illegal repression." This fear was what prompted Khrushchev's famous speech before the Twentieth Party Congress, the speech that launched Russia's "60s generation," the "children of the Twentieth Congress." It was, on the one hand, an expression of idealism and humanity; it was also an expression of the nomenklatura's instinct for self-preservation. For the nomenklatura, the two were essentially identical, indivisible. It was here that the crucial step from a totalitarian dictatorship to an authoritarian regime was taken, and something like Peter III's "Edict on the Rights of the Nobility" proclaimed. This new nobility was primarily concerned with protecting itself, as an unspoken but rigidly enforced understanding was reached, guaranteeing them security of both person and property, sanctity of the home, et cetera. This unwritten Magna Carta marked the starting point of the formation of a stable society.

Once these minimal guarantees of personal safety for the new nobles were firmly in place, something similar began to extend to their subjects (i.e., ordinary Soviet citizens). But once stability set in, once the question of personal safety and security was somewhat, somehow, resolved, the question of private property inevitably came to the fore. The "economic foundation" of socialism began to buckle.

People began to accumulate personal wealth. This was far too modest a process to be called "primitive capital accumulation," but it was certainly a precursor. That is, certain social groups had begun to amass money rather than goods—capital that as yet had no outlet or application. These "precapitalists" were members of the nomenklatura, they were high-level trade and commerce officials, blackmarketeers, generals; they also included a small number of highly successful artists, writers, and performers. Still, not all of these fortunes were so modest. According to one-time Gorbachev assistant A. S. Chernyaev, assets held by Georgy Markov as of 1986 (when Markov chaired the USSR Writers' Union) amounted to nearly 14 million rubles.[16] In terms of 1994 buying power, that is roughly 40–50 billion rubles. Even today few people can boast of having that much personal wealth.

But the mere accumulation of material wealth did not mean so much in itself. Much more significant was the ongoing change in property relations and the fact that the system of managing government property was changing too.

Factory directors, ministers, and other high-level officials who had run their respective enterprises, industries, or regions for a very long time enjoyed a relatively stable position. They had acquired a great deal of money, authority, and influence over the years, and this had significantly changed both their management philosophy and their management practices. By now, these nomenklatura bonzes felt confident enough to take a major step—to shed the role of manager and don that of real owner and proprietor. This wasn't quite privatization, but it was an emerging "sense of ownership" (albeit by those who gave the orders, not by those who followed them).

Once tyranny itself collapsed, so did central management. Formally, the system still stood: the rigidly structured command economy directly subordinate to the Central Committee of the Communist Party, to Gosplan, was still intact. But the reality was different. Powerful enterprise directors, ministers, and regional Party chairmen all wielded informal but considerable autonomous authority. As economist Vitaly Naishul has noted:

> what Russia had was not a command system, but a system of understandings, a complex bureaucratic market built on trade and exchange conducted by both official state agencies and individuals. Unlike the usual money-based market of goods and services, the bureaucratic market traded in not only (and perhaps not primarily) material goods . . . , but in power and rank, rules and exceptions, social position—basically, in anything that had any value at all. Agreement by a factory director to up production norms might be exchanged for, say, increased prestige within the system, or an extra shipment of pipe plus tacit permission to violate some clause in his instruction.[17]

Bureaucratic markets have always existed, and always will. But in normal market economies the bureaucratic market is secondary to a real market, a market where prices are law. To put it another way, the bureaucratic market is what remains of a normal market when there is no such thing as private ownership, when we take the common denominator—money—out of the property relations equation. (To make an analogy: if a person has hearing and speech, gesture and mime are a secondary means of communication. Among the deaf, however, gesture and mime are primary.) In states where the "Asiatic mode of production" prevails, the bureaucratic market does exert at least some control over the system. The dividing line between an authoritarian, "Asiatic," imperial-socialist regime (Lenin) and a totalitarian one (Stalin) lies here: development of a bureaucratic market/suppression of a bureaucratic market.

At this point, state capitalism was still a long way off. But the spring had begun to unwind; the monolith had begun to crack. The faster the bureaucratic market grew, the faster the traders on that market begin to consider themselves an independent social force with its own interests to defend.

Thus, this "pre-civil" society—ugly, shady, semi-criminal, and oligarchic as it was—grew and matured within the greater System, pressuring that system, demanding some kind of change, some kind of lawful outlet for the desire, the opportunity, to manage property freely or even to own it free and clear. The system was ripe for a Thermidor. But this second Thermidor was to take place in a world very different from that of NEP. The new nomenklatura no longer feared a capitalist restoration.

This time, factory directors and high-ranking officials were all supremely confident of their place in society. Unlike their predecessors, they faced no competition from Nepmen, kulaks, or the old intelligentsia. (There was still the black market to contend with, but the nomenklatura could negotiate with it from a position of strength.) Whatever social upheavals might come, they would not automatically benefit any particular social group. If anyone might profit, it was the nomenklatura.

There was one more indicator of just how alienated the nomenklatura was from its parent regime. From the late 1970s on, the Soviet elite (and the Soviet people too) tended to use one word to describe the overall state of the nation. That word was "senility." Even more important than the objective truth of the description was the fact that the nomenklatura recognized it. The nomenklatura was ready for a change.

6

By the late 1970s and early 1980s, only the husk of a system remained, most visibly symbolized by a decrepit, gerontocratic Politburo.

The dread regime feared by everyone, itself fearful of everyone and everything, was holding on out of sheer inertia, shielding itself from the blinding light of reason by hiding its head in the tattered old shawl of ideology and ritual. But ideological ritual had long since lost its original meaning, and any other as well; it had been the butt of jokes even back in the 1930s. And no one made more malicious fun of ritual than did the nomenklatura itself. The reality of regional Party chairmen, Cabinet ministers, and millionaire kolkhoz directors singing revolutionary songs about their life as "hungry slaves," of how "their outraged reason boils and leads them into battle to the death" was far more surreal, vicious, and murderous satire than anything Zhvanetsky or Ionesco could invent. As the poet said: "and like bees in an abandoned hive / the dead words reek of rot."[18] The shroud of ritual incantations that covered Russia, the shroud under which she twitched and tossed, was beginning to give off an unholy stink. To put it another way, people were beginning to see that not only was the emperor naked—the emperor was dead. The third component of the System, the ideological anticapitalist, antiproperty component that had once made the System both coherent and unique, was rotting fastest of all.

In any case, unlike the early Bolsheviks, the nomenklatura of the 1960s–1980s most certainly did not see itself as a band of ruthless Jacobin revolutionaries. The umbilical cord tying them to official Communist antiproperty ideology was barely holding; they were tethered only by their "Party word of honor."

In the 1970s, the "anti-Soviet" alarm raised by Aleksandr Isaevich Solzhenitsyn began resounding ever more loudly. "Stop living a lie!" He called the country's leaders to "[C]ast off this worn-out ideology! . . . Strip off, shake off this sweat-soaked filthy shirt so caked with blood that the living body of the nation cannot breathe."[19]

In essence, the writer was challenging Soviet leaders to secularize the Russian state, to strip the faded, blistered paint of a once sacred ideology from the house of state, to turn a temple into a forum. But what happens if paint is all that keeps the house standing? What if, without that paint, the house will simply collapse? How will this living elite keep living without the dead ideology that sustains it? Will it not end up just as "worn out," just as illegitimate?

The nomenklatura of the 1970s was not ready for radical, global change. However, it was more than ready for small-scale, local changes. I do not believe the tales about Politburo efforts to keep the "hearse races" going as long as possible, by deliberately electing one ancient Party elder after another to the post of Secretary-General. The very speed with which Gorbachev's appointment was announced after Chernenko's death proves that, for once, the official formula "by unanimous vote of the Politburo" actually corresponded to reality. Georgy Arbatov, who in 1985 was visiting New York as a member of a high-level Central Committee delegation, recalled that "everyone said the same thing—that Gorbachev was the only choice, the only one who could lead the nation. They even threatened to stand up and protest at the Party plenum in Moscow if he wasn't chosen." But that was exactly what Party leaders in Moscow thought too, and he was chosen. When the New York delegation heard that the plenum had already taken place and that Gorbachev had been elected, a genuine celebration broke out. I said, half joking, 'Maybe we should put off celebrating until we're on the plane. After all, the nation is supposed to be in mourning!' "[20]

I believe we can take Arbatov at his word here. The nomenklatura (and the rest of the nation too) were waiting for a change, a renewal, and at the time Gorbachev seemed the very man to bring it about.

But change required an ideology to justify it. "Suslov Marxism" aside, there were only two ideologies genuinely popular at the time: one was traditional, national-imperial chauvinism, or "statism"; the other was "socialism with a human face."

The first was backed by long-standing and powerful tradition. It had for centuries been the dominant ideology of Russia, the official ideology, and this dominance by no means ended in 1917. Neither the nominal secularization of the state under Communism nor the death of Communist ideology had undermined it. Communism merely became, once and for all, national-Bolshevism.

By the 1980s, formal descriptions of the ideology consisted of two absolutely disparate components. The content was pure statism (i.e., canonization of "firm" state-authoritarian-bureaucratic rule). The form was pseudo-Marxist ritual and anticapitalist, antiproperty rhetoric.

All that remained was to discard the remnants of the latter, and revive the former. Thus we would cease to "live a lie" but continue a living imperial tradition. In essence, this is the platform of today's "Russian patriots." There were certain psychological overtones accompanying this powerful, unexamined tradition of deifying the state: xenophobia, anti-Semitism, imperial vanity, and hypocrisy. The mighty Soviet military-industrial complex was part and parcel of this tradition. And so, given all of the above, this ideology seemed absolutely guaranteed to win the day.

Easier said than done, even if said logically and convincingly. In the first place, by the mid-1980s, the Cold War and the contest with the American military-industrial complex were already lost—this despite the fact that we had tossed every bit of fuel we had into the boiler of our "armored train." Our insane system made high-tech industries work solely for the "war effort." What was left? Train the entire population of the Soviet Union to wear military issue foot-wraps instead of socks, and eat machine oil instead of food?

But this "great-power Renaissance" was unachievable not only in practical terms, but, much more important, was both unworkable and unprofitable for the budding-capitalist nomenklatura.

Indeed, there was no *logical* connection between the ideology's "great-power" (nationalist) component and its Bolshevik (Communist, antiproperty) one. Logically, the two are easily separable. But there was a historical and psychological connection between the two, dating back to the 1920s and 1930s, when national-Bolshevism emerged as a compromise. Great-power nationalism had grown and developed within the Marxist sac for so long (sixty years) that by now it was forever joined to that ideology, with no strength to shed its Marxist cocoon.

In other words, the only form that triumphant state-imperial ideology could take in the 1980s was national-Bolshevism (equals neo-Stalinism). The nomenklatura took this as yet another "tightening of the screws," which in their case meant a tightening of the purse strings and renewed restrictions on their freedom—especially their freedom to accumulate wealth. Stalinist hard-liners were the chief backers, the chief bearers of this ideology, which enjoyed little popularity either among common folk or the Party elite, the economic elite, or even the military-industrial complex, all of whom were hoping to see their long cherished dreams of ownership come true.

So in fact the victory eventually fell to "socialism with a human face." From the 1960s into the 1980s this "face" was a kind of protective mask, the only one under which a whole conglomerate of disparate ideas could come together: utopian-humanist variations on "early Marx" and "true Marxism" (or even "good Leninism" as opposed to "bad Stalinism"), a range of ideas close to social-democracy or even run-of-the-mill liberalism; most important, the banal notion of a "consumer society" saved from "Marxist senility." The interplay of all these positions, advanced by very different people and very different groups, was very complex. But one common thread ran throughout: rejection of a senile, ossified post-Stalinist ideology and system and an overall "pro-Western" slant.

But what did that mean, precisely? For some, "Western" meant the Prague Spring. For others, it was Eurocommunism, and for yet others, it was the "Swedish model." But for everyone, almost without exception, it meant luxury stores and a comfortable life. That is, very few saw "socialism with a human face" in terms of a consistent political and economic policy that could lead to a stable political and economic system.

And indeed, even if someone had tried to bring together such diverse characters as a Georgian black-market manufacturer looking to expand his business by bribing one local Party secretary and hoping to bribe even more, a Helsinki watch-group consultant, a Central Committee international relations consultant advising the USSR to work for détente, an academic historian trying to sort out the true history of the Communist Party, a foreign-currency fence dreaming of changes in the law, "golden boys" from the State Institute of International Relations ready and willing to beat back capitalism only if they could do so from inside the enemy walls, a general director wanting to manage "his" plant's budget on his own, a foreign trade official casting envious glances at his wealthy Western counterparts (and agreeing to accept the occasional "gift" from them)—if anyone had actually managed to bring all these people together and tell them that all their efforts would ultimately result in the disappearance of all those institutions and organizations of which they were a part, in the rise of political freedoms, free markets, and the capitalism in Russia, they would all have been mightily surprised.

But when the floodgates opened in 1985, that is exactly what happened. And now, when people talk about the overly slow pace, the missed opportunities, the general failure of the Gorbachev-Ryzhkov reforms, they miss the point—the social point, the social target.

If we keep in mind that the point was in fact "nomenklatura privatization," these criticisms are unfair. Reforms were accomplished rather quickly, if sloppily. And only the most paranoid sort of thinking, the search for conspiracies around every corner, could see this process as some "secret plan" to divide up the spoils, as an organized plot to privatize state property. It was nothing of the sort, nor could it have been. The nomenklatura, even at its best, was hardly farsighted enough (let alone unified enough) to concoct or carry out such plans, and once it came to dividing up the spoils, the thought of unified action was inconceivable. No, everything was done as it has always been done throughout history—by process of trial and error. We should note, however, that here it was done rather effectively, in the sense that the bureaucracy profited from the trials, while the state ended up paying for the errors. The nomenklatura was feeling its way into the future, simply putting one foot in front of the other, following its instincts rather than some predetermined plan. It was following the scent of property, a predator after prey.

7

That a revolution launched from above should be taken up by grassroots forces, *and* taken up under the banner of anti-elitism, of egalitarianism, is perfectly natural.

Even as late as 1990 (!) many people did not believe that perestroika was genuine; they saw it as a kind of feint, a maneuver designed to shore up and preserve the traditional Soviet system. Of course such a maneuver would have been an absurdity, considering external factors—the system, the ideology, the empire and everything else recognized as having been imposed on human nature. In reality, what perestroika did was expose the nomenklatura's efforts to perfect its bureaucratic-market system, the search for new names for old things, for new theoretical justifications for bureaucratic rule, all of which required a new facade for this shabby old construct, a legalization of the property relations that had arisen spontaneously within it, a raising (or perhaps an unveiling) of the new building of nomenklatura-bureaucratic-state capitalism. And the only real way to do that was to raise the populist banner.

Such is the usual fate of any revolution that is physically carried out by the masses in the interests, usually, of an organized minority (as a rule, a wealthy and rather privileged one even under the old regime). There is a certain irony here, a Tartuffian turn to revolution—that is, it always promises more than it can deliver. And how many of those democratic activists in 1990 and 1991 later became disillusioned for that very reason, people who, like Yuri Vlasov, even became ferocious opponents of reform?[21]

But in politics, publicly declared goals and actual results will never coincide perfectly, especially in the midst of abrupt turns and revolutionary shifts: the more radical, the more singleminded, the more "honest" and "consistent" a revolution is, the greater the gap between the goals, intentions, and hopes of the masses and the actual outcome. This is all the more true when a revolution turns bloody, when it becomes irreversible. This was a danger in 1990–91, one that we fortunately managed to avoid. Happily, a real revolution (that is, the massively destructive sort that we usually associate with the word) did not take place. And while we might argue terminology (was this a peaceful, "soft" revolution, or was this a radical evolution of the state?), the fact is that the bomb never exploded. I believe that there were a number of reasons why it did not.

The first was the international situation. Europe was at peace. The force field of hatred and aggression that had surrounded, permeated Europe during the First World War—the war that had given birth to Bolshevism—had dissipated. Eastern Europe's "velvet revolutions" had quietly rustled past; even in Rumania the process had stopped short of all-out war. The situation was reminiscent of 1848 with its flurry of "student," democratic, or bourgeois-democratic uprisings; this "wind from the West" undoubtedly had a salutary effect on Russia as well. The most popular (populist, if you will) slogans between 1988 and 1991 were those that shouted for freedom and for markets. In some sense, I suppose, these were the slogans of a "consumer society." And Russian voters naively, or perhaps too impatiently (although their impatience was justified), assumed that these words would suddenly become reality, that they would guarantee Russia the same standard of living that the "civilized world" enjoyed.

The second reason is Russian historical experience. There is some hope that what happened between 1900 and 1953 has inoculated Russia against the application of political terror, against violent revolutions, permanent or transitory either one. At least between 1988 and 1991 no one—no party, no serious political or social force—was willing to call on the Russian people to "take up the axe."

Back in 1969, in an attempt to predict what might transpire after the inevitable collapse of the Soviet system, Andrei Amalrik wrote that "[i]f and when the regime grows weak, mass discontent will lead to horrible consequences. Compared to these, the horrors of the 1905–1907 and 1917–1920 revolutions will look like some pastoral idyll."[22]

This "healthy fear" was in the air in 1988–91, as a radical intelligentsia fanned the flames of discontent, but still kept a firm grip on the fire extinguisher. To switch metaphors, while their grandparents had put the pedal to the metal, these grandchildren always kept one foot on the brake. This same fear hung over most Russian voters. While most people were perhaps ignorant of the historical details, they intuitively sensed one thing—that there was nothing worse than a violent revolution. The "rumors of civil war" sung about by the famous bard Shevchuk, turned out to be nothing more than that.

So in this new Russian revolution, neither the intelligentsia nor the common people chose to play the role of "suicidal extremist."

Here we should acknowledge Boris Yeltsin's sense of political responsibility, as he headed this movement, held it firmly in check, prevented it from breaking out into riot and revolt, guided it toward an orderly transition of power revolutionary in form but compromissary in substance.

Finally, the nomenklatura itself maneuvered rather adeptly. It showed itself to be more flexible than might have been expected. That is, between the nomenklatura and the people there was no iron curtain to tear down; the curtain, by now, was more rubber than iron—which made the use of force ridiculous, and the possibility of a "soft" revolution all the more natural.

Fear and a knowledge of Russian history had so far kept the nomenklatura in check, made it cautious. But the point is that "sidestepping principles" came very easily, since the nomenklatura had never had any in the first place. Party declarations of principle had long since become both odious and ridiculous to the nomenklatura itself. The only real principle remaining was self-interest, and the nomenklatura hardly sidestepped that. Quite the contrary. In the end, what was achieved was this—a decisive but peaceful change of power, evolutionary in essence, revolutionary in form. It is another matter that the compromise regime that emerged from all this is fraught with conflicting interests and potentially dangerous contradictions.

The main question that remains unanswered is this: what sort of order are we building; where are we headed as we leave the "socialist heights"? Are we moving into an free and open Western-type market economy, or into nomenklatura capitalism—that is, yet another variation on Lenin's classic "imperialism" plus Marx's "Asiatic mode of production"?

This is the question that stands before us. This is the choice we must make.

5 Primitive Capital Accumulation

Far socialism, you are so near.
—Boris Pasternak

I

TODAY, WE CAN DRAW SOME PRELIMINARY CONCLUSIONS ABOUT THE
social and economic changes of recent years. If we were to try to reduce
these changes to a single formula, we might say it was simply a swap:
power for private property. It was—and it wasn't. Still, no other formula seems to work here.

Swapping power for private gain might sound less than noble, but
if we are to be realistic, if we are to proceed from the actual alignment
of forces in the late 1980s, this exchange was the only peaceful way for
the society to reform or the state to evolve. The alternative was civil
strife, civil war, and yet another dictatorship—this time a dictatorship
of a new nomenklatura.

Russia could not be wrested from the nomenklatura by force, nor
did she need to be. Her freedom could be bought. That is, if property
was no longer tied to official position, if a truly free market subject to
the laws of competition, a market in which property constantly changed
hands was actually created—this was indeed the optimal solution. It
didn't matter that the nomenklatura had dominated the market so far;
this actually ensured the continuity of property rights. From now on
all would-be owners and proprietors would have to back their claims.

Whatever else it was, this exchange of official position for private property was a step in the right direction: away from "imperialism" and toward a free and open market; away from the Asiatic mode of production; away from a system in which the nomenklatura was a permanent, hereditary political-economic elite immune from the law of markets.

This vision of an exchange of governmental authority for ownership of private property might have suited democratic forces, but the view from the other side was quite different.

Plant managers, high-level ministry officials, high-ranking military and security officers, and district and regional Party secretaries had certainly supported changing the system, and had indeed relinquished some of their administrative power. But they saw the overall equation in entirely different terms. Their equation was this: acquisition of property plus preservation of power. They wanted Russia to turn in the same circles she always had, to stay within her same old magnetic field—safe from market forces.

They wanted to carve up the system (i.e., state property) and take home what they could, but they also wanted to keep intact those parts of the system that guaranteed the primacy of the state. The nomenklatura was like a chick pecking its way out of its shell: inside, life was cramped; outside life was scary.

The nomenklatura was hardly unique in feeling this way. Many people had long dreamed of "very private" ownership, in the sense that they or their clan would own (or manage, or control, or profit from) private holdings, while the state would take care of everyone and everything else. As our famous and eminently successful entrepreneur M. Yuriev has written: "Big business, unlike small or medium business (let alone the rest of the populace) is best served by a semi-laissez-faire economy, which means laissez-faire for the big businessman, but not for anyone else."[1]

So the ideal formula for the bureaucracy was this: power *plus* property! Take the old bureaucratic market wherein the players' positions were defined by government rank and authority, and build the new market on that foundation, meanwhile learning how to extract real cash revenue. In Russian "newspeak" there is a rather precise term for this—

a "regulated market" (regulated by the nomenklatura). The idea was to denationalize in such a way that (paraphrasing Lenin here) production (i.e., the expenses and the risk) remained public, but appropriation became private. The foundations of state monopoly capitalism / imperialism would remain intact. Privatization would not be recognized as official policy, would never be conducted openly, but would nonetheless go on, within the inner circle, "just for us."

The first stage would look roughly like this: control over property would remain in state (bureaucratic) hands, but the state would ease its control over the bureaucrats themselves, then eventually give it up entirely. In other words, state officials would still wield enormous power to manage and distribute resources, just as they always had. However, within the state system, within the inner circle, they could now shed their verbal camouflage and openly speak the language of the market. They could haggle with selected business partners over financial (low-interest loans) and natural (quotas, licenses) resources now at their disposal; they could dicker over "their" capital funds and product. The economist who coined the term "administrative-command system" once proposed that government officials officially and legally be paid a "margin" (i.e., a commission) on each commercial or financial transaction closed. Apparently this is how he envisioned creating markets "within the system."[2] If by "officially" he meant openly and publicly, the nomenklatura would never have agreed. But if "officially" were to mean "according to strictly defined rules and rates," the nomenklatura would have agreed in a minute. This was their dream.

Thus the ideal solution took shape: as far as "mode of appropriation" went, state officials were owners, capitalists, "proprietors." But in terms of actual responsibility they were neither capitalists nor traditional civil servants. Civil service as such no longer existed. If we add in yet another factor, all the offshoots of state enterprises (cooperatives, TOOs, small and medium-sized businesses owned and controlled by the families and friends of the directors, by organizations whose economic raison d'être was generating cash and laundering money), it was a perfectly ingenious solution. The road to riches was wide open: no one was accountable for anything. With the master long gone, the bureaucrats were now the "stewards"—"state employees" of a paralyzed state.

It was all quite simple. The old bureaucratic market would operate as it always had, but meanwhile, subordinate to it, a normal economic market would gradually be created. However, this latter would play an auxiliary role only: it would "launder" money; it would help in the ongoing process of converting administrative powers into actual wealth. Essentially, it would be a command economy that had learned how to exploit the market—or rather, one that had created its own market to exploit.

There was nothing especially new in all this. It is instructive to compare this market structure with Yuri Larin's 1927 description of NEP era markets. As he lists twelve types of illegal capitalist activity, he is careful to delineate one key factor—the presence of "accomplices" and "agents" within the government itself.

> Within the state apparatus there was a rather small, rather limited and measurable group of people (ten, twenty, thirty thousand) who used their positions in government agencies to set up various businesses and register them to relatives, companions, or sometimes even to themselves. They would then cycle government funds allocated to their respective departments into these private enterprises. Once that transfer was accomplished, they would usually leave government service to "stand on their own two feet."

Further, Larin writes:

> By the term "pseudo-state private capital," I mean a setting in which private entrepreneurs grow and expand their own businesses while nominally remaining in state service, all the while wielding state authority. In essence, what we have here is an agreement between a private vendor, a private contractor, or a private manufacturer, and a governmental body. Formally, however, this vendor, this contractor, this manufacturer, etc. are all government servants acting not on behalf of themselves, but on behalf of the agency they represent . . . In a word, they enjoy all the advantages accruing to a government agency, but are in reality private entrepreneurs who merely contract with government agencies.[3]

In 1923, the total amount of private capital held by these "tens of thousands" was estimated to be about 350 million gold rubles. In today's terms that would be approximately five trillion. The amount of private capital in Russia today is considerably greater. But while the numbers may be different, the mechanism of capital formation is described fairly accurately. From 1988 on, an ever-growing part of the economy has taken this form, and within just a few years this form has come to dominate.

Gradually, step by step, by around 1990 we had arrived at the very state of affairs Larin described in 1927. Each of these steps had brought more and more perquisites to the nomenklatura. Some milestones along the way included the enactment of the law on cooperatives, on the election of enterprise directors, a marked reduction in these directors' accountability to their relative ministries (this along with the virtual disappearance of the traditional Party discipline that had kept them all in line), and finally, a change in regulations—thanks to which enterprises were now able to "crank up" both salaries and prices even though prices had not yet officially been freed. In my view, the "late-Ryzhkov, early-Pavlov" period of 1988–91 was in fact the golden age of these elite political-economic groups. It is no coincidence that the foundations of most of the major firms (and fortunes) that now dominate the Russian economy were laid in those very years.

Certain social groups suddenly became very, very rich: some (but not all) high-ranking officials and factory directors, managers of "selected" cooperatives that had for one reason or another received government funding, plus the movers and shakers of "Komsomol, Inc." These were the people who had taken their initial capital and rushed to create "independent banks," to capture (or in some cases create) highly profitable markets.

It should be noted that these "pioneers" constituted a rather closed group; their watchword might have been "outsiders need not apply." Of course, during a get-rich boom, trying to seal off all access is simply not realistic, nor was it realistic to think that the old nomenklatura could, without breaking formation, simply move to the front ranks of the new market elite, march in, and occupy the emerging market. Nonetheless they largely managed to do just that, thanks to firm administrative controls on "allocation" of privileges (i.e., fortunes). In any event, the "big money" did not essentially change hands after 1991. The economic elite that had emerged by that time was proving to be rather stable. Meanwhile, on a parallel track, a political elite was also emerging: this mix included the "reconstructed" nomenklatura as well as some other groups who had decided to take their chances in the big lottery—Russia's very first free elections.

It is worth mentioning that in spite of all the recent wailing and lamentation in the press, the scale of nomenklatura theft and embezzlement was far greater in 1990–91 than it is now. Between 1992 and 1994 we have seen a number of financial scandals (Urozhay-90 checks, for example), but nothing truly significant.[4] There have always been financial scandals and there always will be. The problem has been the system itself: complete ambiguity around property rights, absolute lack of accountability, two power centers (the Kremlin and the Russian White House for the nation as a whole, the Kremlin and local authorities for the "outlying" republics), all of which seemed to have been created (and perhaps were?) to allow a particular group of people to fearlessly and unabashedly make themselves rich. The nomenklatura emerged from perestroika into a "neutral zone," a no man's land where it could do absolutely anything it wanted, and where it hoped to stay as long as it could.

In 1990 and 1991 it was popular to vilify Lenin, but it was precisely in those years that his description of state monopoly capitalism (imperialism) as "predatory, parasitic, and decaying" was so brilliantly borne out. Post-Communist imperialism had worked so perfectly that the country was now on the brink of economic collapse.

Such was the price of a spontaneously struck historical compromise. The nomenklatura had been building capitalism for its own profit, by its own measure, at its own pace. This was precisely what made it possible for the entire country (including those factions who declared themselves to be anti-elite and pro-democracy) to cover a great deal of necessary ground on its inevitable road to the market.

By the end of 1991 we had a hybrid market—part bureaucratic, part economic (the former still dominant). And thanks to fundamental legal ambiguity on property rights, nomenklatura capitalism was all but complete.

Pseudostate capital activity reigned. In politics we also had a hybrid: a combination of Soviet and presidential forms of rule, a post-Communist but pre democratic republic.

And while the ruling classes seemed to be well on the way to solving their own problems, the overall economy was falling apart. The volume of goods manufactured in 1991 was double that of today (1994), but shelves remained empty. Soviet currency was worthless, orders were left unfilled, a sense of impending doom was in the air: the talk was of starvation and cold, transportation systems paralyzed, a country in ruins.

2

And so "emergency reforms" began, and the "kamikaze" team was brought in.

We were called because a choice had to be made. Up until that moment, nomenklatura privatization had been evolving in the classic "Asiatic mode"; that is, the satraps had been steadily, quietly, and discreetly plundering their own satrapies. In medieval times this process could drag on for decades; in modern Russia it took a mere three years (1989 through 1991) to empty the well. Still, the basic features were the same: covert, parasitic privatization on the one hand; no market and no change in forms of ownership on the other. Officially, as of 1 January 1992, Russia had privatized 107 retail stores, 58 cafeterias and restaurants, and 36 service establishments. In reality—in terms of real control over property, in terms of profit, etcetera—virtually the entire economy had been privatized. However, the country was teetering on the edge of ruin. Even the nomenklatura understood this perfectly well; it lived in and off "this country" after all, and was therefore willing to make certain concessions—small ones, at least. In "Eastern" societies this sort of privatization had always ended in an outburst of violence followed by a new dictatorship. The cycle of social development had always looked like this: dictatorship → disintegration (privatization) → violence → a new dictatorship. Now the bomb was ticking in Russia too. Paradoxically, just when public faith in democratic government was at its height, we were closer than ever to that dangerous point when "impending catastrophe" and "the need to defend ourselves against it" would require the application of all too familiar measures.

While we understood the gravity of the situation, we also understood that we had a choice. There were two ways out of the wretched excess of bureaucratic rule: an outbreak of violence followed by yet another dictatorship; or a deliberate move to a free and open market; a flip of the switch from covert nomenklatura privatization to overt democratic privatization, from state monopoly capitalism to "open" capitalism. We chose the latter.

Throughout 1991 the exchange of state power for private property had proceeded for the most part along the nomenklatura's chosen "Asiatic" path. In 1992, as real reform began, this process took a different road.

The freeing of prices, the executive order on freedom of trade, the convertible ruble, the beginnings of regulated privatization—what did all these mean in socioeconomic terms?

First of all, they meant that without using force or declaring a state of emergency, we had managed by late 1991 to introduce some small change into property relations and into the disastrous system itself.

In principle, I am a staunch advocate of the combined approach: rigidly defined strategic goals, and flexible tactics for achieving them. The policy we pursued in early 1992 is one example. Our goal was clear: to bring the economy back under control by introducing objective organizational principles into the existing system. Only one move was possible, and that was to let the objective laws of economics work to limit the excesses rampant at the time. Tactically this was a "soft" means of control, in that it did not upset the established balance of social forces. No enterprise directors, no ministerial officials were removed from office, no accounts were seized, no business correspondence confiscated; official positions, funds, and connections remained intact. Henceforth they would be held in check not by administrative whim, but by the law of the market, the law of prices. When the "fans on the sidelines" tell me that we should never have freed prices without a preliminary demonopolization, I want to pose them a question of my own: just how do they envision demonopolization in an economy that has no market, where there are *no* laws—neither administrative nor economic—in force?

Let me quote a newspaper article in which my thoughts on the launching of reforms are fairly clearly laid out:

> We began these reforms in the midst of a rather interesting situation—we could have spent a long time listing what we didn't have and why we shouldn't embark on any reforms at all. I myself could have made a perfectly good case for why we could not, *should* not have begun reforms in 1992. There was no real support for them in the Russian parliament, there were no state institutions capable of real action. . . . everyone and everything was caught up in the early 1990s government crisis. We had six-teen central banks instead of one, we had no tradition of private enterprise, we had a far weaker private sector than a country like Poland. We had not one kopeck in foreign currency, no gold reserves, no way to pull resources in from the international finan-cial market. But over and above all that—we had no time to wait around, do nothing at all, and then explain to everyone why we hadn't, and couldn't.[5]

Liberalizing prices was an important step in our move from nomen-klatura freedom to market necessity. Pseudostate ownership, the fig leaf covering nomenklatura ownership, was beginning to slip. Plant direc-tors and other highly placed officials were still using their revenues as they pleased, still free from any official administrative responsibility, but market laws had begun to do their work, and could no longer be ignored. Bankruptcy law did not exist at the time (and even now exists more in form than in substance). But employees had to be paid. Suddenly the bosses were faced with real financial issues.

Money was replacing hierarchical position; money was becoming the true coin of the realm. A normal monetary system was starting to replace the old system, which had consisted mainly of printing and dis-tributing rubles "per special order."

This open, overt privatization was a historical turning point. It was the peaceful, civilized equivalent of revolution. And that is why it bears closer investigation.

3

It was clear from the start that the most important factors to be taken into account in designing a privatization program for Russia had to include the following:

First, the scale of the task ahead was unprecedented. Substantial changes had to be made in a very short time in order to buttress the coming liberalization and stabilization measures with a property structure and an adequate market economy.

Second, Russia's legitimate private sector was very weak. Legitimate private business had only begun to sprout in the latter years of perestroika; capital accumulated during this time had no historical legitimacy in the minds of the public. People automatically assumed a close connection between new business and the old shadow economy.

Third, foreign capital could play only a limited role in privatization. Given the size of our economy and the socioeconomic risks involved, it was obviously unrealistic to count on massive foreign investment in Russian privatization.

Fourth, unlike the rest of Eastern and Central Europe, we did not have to deal with claims made by former property owners. Russia's long history of socialism removed the issue of restitution.

Considering all of the above, our solutions were essentially a given.

First, we had to reject the individual approach to privatization: that is, we would not attempt to reorganize individual enterprises before we had redefined property relations overall. We had instead to focus on the application of universal procedures and standard rules, thus making the process less dependent on decisions made by individual managers or directors.

Second, we had to focus on creating privatization coalitions that would allow us to launch this massive process from the ground up rather than from the top down; we had to strive to integrate the interests of those social groups and political forces capable of paralyzing the process if they felt excluded (employees, heads of enterprises, regional governmental bodies, etc.).

Third, we had to eschew any large-scale attempts to combine privatization and the recapitalization of enterprises, and work instead to create effective property-ownership structures.

Fourth, we had to work to ensure the right of all Russian citizens to acquire the property now being privatized; we also had to work to create additional demand for such property.

By the end of December 1991, the platform of a privatization program based on the above principles had been discussed by the Yeltsin government, ratified by presidential order, and sent to the Supreme Soviet for confirmation. A powerful new federal agency began to take shape; it had to be capable of handling the far from simple organizational and legal challenges ahead. I consider it tremendously fortunate that Anatoly Chubais, perhaps the most talented organizer and administrator on our team, took on the task of spearheading this enormous effort. A broad range of experts, Russian and foreign alike, were recruited to draft the scores of regulatory documents necessary. In February 1992 a trial run was held: there were auctions aimed at privatizing trade and service industries. In March, after a slow start and considerable resistance, privatization of small businesses began to gather momentum not only in Moscow but in outlying regions of Russia as well. Attempts by public trade sector employees to stir up public outcry against the auctions by claiming that they threatened the sacred rights of the "employee collective" met with little support. In a deficit economy, most people had learned the hard way just what those "sacred rights" were worth.

We proceeded from the assumption that we could not expect optimal economic solutions. Indeed, what in the long term proves optimal economically may be what in the short term seems merely socially acceptable and sustainable. This assumption lay at the heart of the privatization program that Yeltsin's "kamikaze team," exhausting any political capital the reform movement still had, pushed through the Supreme Soviet in the spring of 1992.

A number of privatization plans were proposed in an effort to address the claims of a variety of groups: employees (sale of some shares at residual cost), directors (options for heads of enterprises), local governing bodies (privatization revenues funneled into regional budgets), and ordinary citizens employed in other sectors of the economy (privatization checks, or vouchers). It was a working compromise, far from ideal, but one that allowed for a wide-reaching, orderly redistribution of property—that is, one that would clear the way for market mechanisms that would effectively distribute it.

During debate in the Supreme Soviet, one group, however, managed to tip the scales. A new variation on privatization was introduced, a plan under which employees, as a collective, were allowed to buy 51 percent of the shares of their enterprise at residual cost. This was a blow to ordinary citizens, because by adopting this measure the Supreme Soviet was making privatization vouchers essentially worthless before they had even been issued. Even more important, this plan meant that, once privatized, Russian enterprises would simply become a typical "industrial kolkhoz." Supreme Soviet restrictions on the reappraisal of the property purchased at residual cost would reduce any possible revenues from privatization.

The government was faced with a choice. It could dig in its heels, stand on principle, insist on the original legislation—and thus slow down the entire process of reapportioning property. Or it could agree to the changes, realizing all the while that the resulting property structure would be far from optimal. Losing momentum at this point was something the government could not afford. Its decision to go ahead and launch this far from perfect program would in large part determine the further development of economic reforms in Russia.

Initially, privatization legislation had not stipulated the introduction of any form of cash payment, of a "voucher." The government had initially proposed the creation of a system of personal privatization accounts through which it would then operate.

But it became clear at the very outset that any attempt to put such a system in place would be fraught with enormous practical problems. First we would need to create another bank system parallel to the already existing system of savings banks; creating and establishing this parallel network would require tremendous investment, enormous amounts of time and money. This would mean putting off property structure reform for at least another year. The choice was extremely simple. We could start laying the groundwork for a new banking system and miss our window of opportunity, our one real historical chance to begin the process of property distribution, or we could find another way around the problem, and move ahead.

The trouble with many of the privatization programs implemented in Eastern Europe and the former Soviet republics was that the "tools of privatization" were not liquid. As soon as people realized that they had been handed something that could neither be bought nor sold, they assumed that the whole process was a farce. Therefore it was essential that our privatization checks be tradable, liquid. And this is what made our voucher a working tool.

The question of what denomination to put on the voucher was really rather abstract. This was a document attesting to an individual's right to acquire privatized property, and the real value of the voucher did not depend on the number written on it; its value was largely social and psychological. The monetary value would be determined by the amount of the privatized property, by the financial stability of the enterprise, by benefits accorded to employees. In the end, for simplicity's sake, we settled on 10,000 rubles.

We understood perfectly well that the psychology of the 148 million people about to receive vouchers would not suddenly change once they had those vouchers in hand, that they would not suddenly start seeing themselves as owners and proprietors. Yet the voucher was a tool that allowed us to change the mechanism of property distribution in Russia. It will take decades for an "ownership mentality" to develop in our country. It cannot and could not be created by fiat. But what the decision to issue vouchers could do was create a market for private property. And therein lay the real meaning of privatization.

Behind-the-scenes privatization, privatization for the nomenklatura alone, was over. Yes, granted, the property market was hardly equitable or even fully open. One wave of the wand cannot undo all the ties between property and government office—nor should it, just as we need not and should not try to forcibly eliminate existing notions about the legitimacy of certain property rights. Privatization itself creates an easy, flexible mechanism for change of ownership—or at least the possibility of such a mechanism.

What does it matter if the first stage of privatization leaves "industrial kolkhozes" under the command of their previous directors, who for all practical purposes were, and are, their true owners? The résumés of people who trade on a market do not determine whether it is "nomenklatura" or "free." "Résumé racism" (that is, when people are defined as "good" or "bad" depending on which boxes they have checked off under race, ethnic background, previous position, etc.) is in any case both odious and senseless. A market dominated by former members of the Soviet nomenklatura is not automatically a nomenklatura market, nor is privatization under which former members of the elite can own property the same as nomenklatura privatization. This is not a question of individuals, but of a system; we are not talking about actors, but about roles and rules in the theater of economics. We are talking about which rules will henceforth govern our markets. Will these be transparent, written rules subject to the laws of economics, of free competition, or will they be the same old secret, administrative, "telephone" rules delimited by official relationships, rules designed for a state-bureaucratic machine? These are the criteria for defining a nomenklatura market versus a free market, for differentiating between nomenklatura privatization and market privatization. Again, just because former members of the nomenklatura enter a free-market system and begin to play by that system's rules, the market itself does not automatically become a nomenklatura market. Nor does a bureaucratic market automatically become a democratic one just because former dissidents begin to occupy positions of authority and to play by that market's rules.

Privatization changed the legal framework of property relations; it eroded the entire nomenklatura-bureaucratic "power market." The nomenklatura itself has been privatized. Now it will have to play by real market rules; bureaucratic *krugovaya poruka* has either collapsed or been greatly undermined. Of course the system that has recently taken shape is a transitional one. We have completed the first stage of privatization, but if in stage two recently enacted bankruptcy laws begin to take effect, if shares controlled by the state are sold on a broad scale, if a secondary securities market emerges, if an ongoing process of pure market exchange and redistribution of property continues to move forward, the changes we have already seen will become irreversible, and Russia will move out of nomenklatura capitalism, away from a mixed but largely bureaucratic market, away from pseudostate property, and move toward a truly free market and truly private ownership. The privatization process of 1992–94 has been a necessary and crucial step on this path.[6]

4

There was no real "shock therapy" in 1992, nor in the years that followed. Knocking down inflation turned out to be an uneven process, with many fits and starts, and little consistency—all in all a painful process. But to fully understand the difference between "nomenklatura" capitalism and "semidemocratic" capitalism, we have only to compare two three-year periods: 1989 through 1991 and 1992 through 1994.

The first period was marked by a relatively modest downturn in production and a relatively mild increase in rates of inflation. Meanwhile the economy was headed inexorably, hopelessly, toward collapse. The standard of living for the vast majority of Russians continued to drop as the nomenklatura continued to accumulate fabulous wealth, generally by plundering state property. Hence social and political tensions grew by leaps and bounds.

The second period saw the overall drop in production become apparent; prices and inflation rates rose sharply as well. Economic wounds were now being laid bare, but from this moment on it became possible to treat them rather than "conjure" over them. True, the standard of living for most of the population was still dropping, but the situation had already begun to change. More and more people were being drawn into the orbit of a "semifree" market, and many of them (especially the young and energetic ones) were beginning to feel some hope, to see some light at the end of the tunnel. The society itself had changed: instead of a few hundred or a few thousand or even a few hundred thousand "selected" people directly engaged in commerce, we now had millions, tens of millions. This is the seed out of which will grow not a new class of millionaires, but a true middle class. And it is this "invisible hand of the market," not some OMON club,[7] that will knock out the "intransigent opposition," (however ugly and fistlike the hand might seem at the moment). State capitalism (socialism) and its cannibalistic economy are changing.

Analysis of recent economic changes in Russia and the newly independent states of the former USSR and Warsaw Pact leads to some paradoxical conclusions which, on their face, are difficult to explain. In all these states, production levels have dropped—and dropped drastically. At the same time, their consumer markets, which were in shambles at the time reforms actually began, have grown. Budget surveys showed that consumption has risen across the board; so has the availability of a wide variety of goods. This was obvious not only to the statistically enhanced eyes of professional economists: it was obvious by the way people were dressed, by the number of cars on the streets. (We are not talking about just Mercedes, by the way. The overall number of passenger vehicles in Moscow more than doubled between 1992 and 1994.) It was obvious in the mass availability of once hard-to-get consumer goods. Production numbers seem to have little to do with people's daily lives.

In Belarus, which had adopted a policy of slow, "regulated" entry into the market, industrial output dropped less than in other countries. But in the summer of 1994 the average salary was still twenty dollars a month. In Estonia and Latvia, where classic "shock therapy" had been applied, production dropped off even more sharply. But there, salaries have been averaging between 110 and 125 dollars per month.

Between January 1992 and August 1994, official statistics for Russia showed a drastic drop in industrial output. At the same time, they showed a gradual increase in retail trade, in real income and personal savings for the population at large. They also showed a positive trade balance and a growth in foreign currency reserves. In normal market economies such a thing would be impossible, and of course we cannot expect this to last for long. But it is instructive, in any case, to investigate the reasons for such a paradox.

The fantastically deformed nature of the socialist economy has actually made reforming it somewhat easier. If there was any link between the standard of living of the average Egyptian peasant and the achievements of the Pharaohs in building the pyramids, it was that the two were inversely proportionate to one another. Under socialism, economic activity that made absolutely no sense in terms of public welfare rose to levels that archaic Eastern despots could only dream of, as socialism erected massive twentieth century industrial "pyramids."

Arms production was the technological, economic, and social

lynchpin of Soviet industry, while the civilian sector was reduced to being a mere subsidiary. The defense industry was the largest consumer of high-grade steel and non-ferrous metals, chemicals, and electronic equipment. By the end of the 1980s the absurdity of what was going on was hard to ignore: the country was sinking ever deeper into debt, the government was squandering its gold and foreign currency reserves, the consumer market was falling apart, food supplies were ever more dependent on imported products and loans that the USSR humbly begged from the West, and meanwhile the military-industrial complex continued to prepare for war against the rest of the world.

Sharp reductions in arms production not only allowed us to break this vicious cycle and create the preconditions for economic recovery, but also served as a catalyst for an industrial crisis in our supermilitarized economy, thus making the painful process of restructuring arms production inevitable.

Our hypertrophied defense sector is the most vivid example— although not the only one— of large-scale economic activity that made no sense in terms of public welfare. The USSR had always lagged behind the United States in agricultural production. Attempts were made to compensate for the profound crisis in agriculture (brought about by the fatal inability of Soviet kolkhozes and sovkhozes to supply the country adequately) by pouring more and more resources into this sector. Overall, by 1985—the peak year of "stable socialism"—we were producing 1.5 times as much fertilizer as the United States, five times as many tractors, sixteen times as many harvesting combines, and meanwhile our dependency on American grain imports continued to grow. It is all too easy to imagine the actual quality of all those tractors and combines, to imagine just how efficiently they were used, all too easy to understand that equipment produced in such quantity was impossible to sell for real money. Mountains of painted scrap—this is what the work of thousands of metallurgists, miners, chemists, engineers, energy experts, and transportation experts turned into.

One well-known example of large-scale, unproductive economic activity reminiscent of the cyclopean projects of Eastern empires was late socialism's attempts at land reclamation. Between 1970 and 1985 the number of square kilometers of irrigated land in the Russian Republic

doubled; in 1985 alone twice as much money was poured into melio-
ration projects as was invested in production of consumer goods (Group
B). No one was ever able to show any positive results—increased
efficiency in agricultural production, for example. Taking the market
track meant unavoidable cuts in these projects, which in turn led to a
drop in demand for cement, reinforced concrete, construction and railroad equipment, and the metals and fuels needed to produce the latter.

The postsocialist Russian economy is having tremendous difficulty
freeing itself from the enormous burden of all this senseless economic
activity, but it is finally beginning to stand on its feet rather than on its
head. Progress here is an absolutely crucial prerequisite for curbing
inflation and stabilizing the economy in general.

At the same time, saturating the market with consumer goods is
not an end in itself. If the deficit is erased by applying the "oil for
Snickers" principle, we will have an internally dismantled, parasitic system that cannibalizes our natural resources—yet another version of the
"pyramid economy" built atop a volcano—and there is no way to tell
when the volcano might become active again.

In this sense, our opponents' outcries over the "colonization" and
destruction of Russian technology, etcetera, have some merit. But, as
always, they merely point out an obvious problem, and then offer the
obviously wrong solution.

Essentially, the problem is clear enough: we must gradually revive
our restructured manufacturing base. This and this alone will lay a firm
foundation for future prosperity; it is and must be Russia's first priority. This is Russia's chance to join the First World.

On this point, general agreement reigns. The argument begins when
we move to the next point. *How* do we reach that prosperity?

5

Going into great economic detail is not really possible here, but in answer
to the question posed above, we should consider the following.

Theoretically, an economy has two sources of funding—state and
private. Clearly, current conditions dictate that both will be used. But
in what proportion?

The continued focus on state funding in modern Russia is a dead-end proposition for three reasons: in the short term, it puts an unbearable burden on the country; it is economically ineffective; in the long term, it merely shores up an already deformed socioeconomic structure.

The state has essentially only one source of revenue—taxation. (This of course includes seignorage, i.e., revenue from the issue of money from taxes on monetary assets.) Still, one of the few facts generally acknowledged by everyone in Russia today, by Communists and liberals alike, is that the tax burden has reached its limit. Any attempt to increase it would lead to mass tax evasion, a retreat into semi-legal, "shadow" business, and reduction in real budget revenue. The hard lessons of our neighbors in Ukraine and Belarus, who have tried moving in this direction, are all too clear and obvious. Solving present problems inherited from a socialist past (everything from supporting social services for displaced workers to cleaning up after the Chernobyl disaster) costs a great deal. Long-term financial analysis convincingly demonstrates that there is virtually no hope of using tax revenues to fund massive state support for manufacturing.

Nation-states are not good at handling money. There is no need to go into lengthy explanations why: suffice it to say that their funds are handled by a bureaucracy relatively unconcerned about either short-term or long-term effects for the country as a whole. The bureaucracy is, however, quite concerned about its own "commission" in any transaction.

This financing system serves to preserve and to reproduce the parasitic structure of a pseudostate economy. As bureaucratic credit circulates in a bureaucratic market in order to maintain bureaucratic privilege. Money flows to the biggest and least efficient concerns, to military-industrial "latifundia." Loans of this sort are less like water for a starving plant than like a desert storm, an inflationary storm in an economic desert dotted by crumbling industrial pyramids. Meanwhile, in the rest of the world, experience seems to have shown that the most economically efficient and technologically progressive firms are not the old industrial giants, but small and medium businesses with a single, clearly designated owner or owners (no more than two or three). It is the aggregate, the totality, of millions of such firms that will make up the flesh and blood of a growing Russian economy. Hence any opportunity for economic growth in Russia is directly related to the scale of private investment.

It is too early to write the history of initial capital accumulation in Russia; the process is ongoing. As elsewhere, it began with import and export transactions, financial speculation, with real estate and commerce.

This capital, including that issuing from the golden foam of inflation and speculation, cannot lie around in anyone's safe for long. Russian capital's natural application is to be found not in Switzerland, but Russia herself. Capital is always seeking an outlet, an application, a means by which to grow.

In order for this capital—that already formed, as well as that in the process of formation—to work in Russia, to become the fermenting agent for growth, two conditions must be met: Russia must have a stable currency, and she must also have reliable guarantees of the sanctity of private property, regardless of the owner's resources inside the state apparatus or outside the law. Property ownership must be made separate from state authority; even more difficult, state authority, (i.e., the bureaucracy) must be separated from "its" property.

Clear-cut legal protections for private property, enforcement of those protections by the state, the support of powerful, well-organized political structures willing to defend private property against threat of confiscation—today these are less a matter for ideological reflection than they are real-life demands, crucial prerequisites for economic growth. If those prerequisites can be created, Russia, with her boundless opportunities for effective capital investment, will begin to move along a path of dynamic economic growth. If over the next several years the legal principle of the sanctity of private property is upheld, it will become simply standard behavior, will be internalized, will become a social and psychological principle rather than a legislated one.

The problem caused by lack of effective protections for private property is especially visible in the economically depressed regions of the so-called Red Belt, where grave institutional problems are dragging down the standard of living, strengthening the Communist position, creating a favorable climate for a bureaucratic market, and frightening away private investors.[8] The result is a vicious cycle: economic depression → lack of property guarantees → lack of private capital investment → economic depression. Essentially, the question is whether we can pull Russia out of this cycle.

The second necessary condition is curbing inflation and stabilizing the currency. Only under this condition will long-term investment make any sense, in manufacturing or any other sector.

In terms of political and social strategy, the link between these two problems is clear enough. If we count mainly on the state, we count on state investment, which means we can count on inflation, which is the inevitable consequence of insufficient state revenues (fatal for private business and a state economy, but not for a bureaucracy). We can also count on legal instability within the private sector, the state's "competitor." That is, in terms of sociology, if we ask the question "Cui bono?"—the answer is obvious. The economy will be caught in the same vicious cycle. Money will flow through the same old bureaucratic channels to the same old manufacturing giants (first and foremost to the military-industrial complex, the guarantor of state proprietorship) to the nomenklatura that still runs them, to the financial barons. Moreover, since there is no such thing as "nobody's" money, all this will have to be underwritten by taxes, including an inflationary tax on personal savings and on small and medium-size businesses; it will be financed by money pumped out of the barely emerging middle class to float a select portion of the upper class, by the impoverishment of the middle class for the enrichment of one small part of the elite.

The result will be economic stagnation and social and political unrest, and another step down the road to the Third World. This outcome will eventually prove fatal to the bureaucratic elite itself, which wields power *here,* lives and gains its wealth *here,* in this country. But those who are hot in pursuit of immediate, personal "tactical gains" will hardly stop for fear of some overall strategic defeat.

If the conditions for stabilizing property ownership (money ownership included) are at least minimally met, then all this capital, obedient to the law of equilibrium, will flow naturally to those points where it will be most effective. Given Russia's natural resources and manufacturing base, one need not be a professional economist to see how many such points there are. By "all this capital" I mean not only the money turned over in financial operations inside Russia, but also those billions of "Russian dollars" sitting in Western banks, as well as major Western capital in search of application.

An economic upswing (or an economic crisis, for that matter) is more or less a chain reaction. If a critical mass of capital is invested, if massive renewal of principal begins, if prosperity grows, then new capital begins to stream in, flowing to the "growth zone." Such is the law of the market.

A genuine upturn in the economy would mean a change in the very structure of our society, the long awaited birth of a middle class—those millions of owners of small private firms who alone can create true markets, dynamic industry, economic growth.

I am convinced that our society lives by this hope. The naive euphoria of early perestroika is gone; gone is the belief that as soon as Russia was rid of the Communists it would automatically become a consumer-capitalist heaven. People have matured. They are willing to work (not demonstrate, not revolt) in order to lead a normal life. No matter how gloomy the responses to various polls and surveys may seem, I am certain that most people, consciously or not, expect better times in the near future, and that this is what is holding our society together.

But they cannot sustain that hope forever. If production does not increase soon, and with it the real standard of living, if the opposite happens and the country enters into another long period of stagnation, the public will soon exhaust its "last reserves of optimism" (the first ones ran out in 1991) and, again feeling itself betrayed, may very well explode in self-destructive, suicidal revolt. Or, far more likely, it will sink into profound apathy.

Neither alternative bodes well for anyone but the extremists. And if they manage to seize power, we are guaranteed a national disaster.

For the moment, there is no apathy in Russia. By that I mean not political apathy, but social apathy—a far more serious condition. People are socially, economically, active; they are working hard. One of the great victories of recent years has been this awakening: people have come out of the lethargic daze characteristic of the workplace under Brezhnev and earlier leaders. True, much of their energy has been directed toward commerce and service, industries generally neglected in the old socialist society. But in any case, this change is one of the things that has ameliorated our socioeconomic and political crisis.

If our society loses its energy and its hope, our nation will indeed begin to sink into a Third World morass. All the building materials we have accumulated with so much effort will only serve as fuel to the fire. Russian civilization is much more stable than the political scientists who earn their living on predictions of gloom and doom would like to believe, but there is a limit to what any structure will bear. The choice between a bureaucratic market (stagnation) and a free market (economic and social development) is, in essence, the choice of Russia's future. Will she hold her place among the world's great civilizations or will she slip into the Third World?[9]

6 The Choice

We know what lies now in the balance
We know what now awaits us.
The hour for courage has struck on our clocks,
And courage will not forsake us.

Anna Akhmatova

I

TODAY, OUR NATION FACES A CHOICE. THIS IS THE ONE THING WE
all seem to agree on, and indeed our opponents seem to be the ones
making the most noise about it. The choice comes down to this: which
of all our competing strategies will keep us from devolving into a third-
rate power; which will stave off economic stagnation and endemic
poverty? Which strategy will put an end to the "Russian economic
miracle"—that is, the wonder of how a country so rich in natural and
human resources has managed to remain so poor for so long. Which
strategy will allow Russia to develop as a normal, First World nation?

It's the same old Russian problem: "We lag behind the leading nations
of the world by fifty to one hundred years. We must make up this distance in ten. Either we do this, or they crush us."

And the same old solution: "We need a state with both the will and
the power to channel these enormous natural riches to the people's
benefit. We need a party cohesive and unified enough that it can direct
all its efforts . . . toward a single goal . . . [unified enough] to steer a
steady course through these difficulties and systematically enforce the
right . . . policy."[1]

So said Stalin in 1931. Peter the Great might have said the same some two centuries earlier. Our self-declared statists, our so-called patriots are saying the same thing today, with only slight adjustments for time and terminology.

Can it be that the true lesson of history is that no one learns any lessons at all? Can it be that Russia's tragic history of "great leaps," her inevitable, mathematically predictable, irreversible failures, her repeated losses of 50–100 years of hard-won ground, have taught us nothing?

The very notion that "robust government efforts" aimed at reinforcing the "Asiatic state" and further developing the "Asiatic mode of production" will permit us to "not only catch up with, but overtake" self-sustaining societies is absurd.

It is not a matter of technology or economic capacity. We have both in abundance. It is a matter of socioeconomic structure. This is the gap we must bridge, the distance we must cover. We must become a nation whose economy is driven not by forced mobilization, but by innovation and change. Bridging this gap requires political will—the will to develop the nation by changing the function of the state.

I will refrain from repeating what has so often been said about Russia's "special destiny," about the East-West split that still runs through our political and governmental consciousness. But lately, what once seemed political abstractions and "salon theories" are once again turning into very real political priorities and decisions.

What should the aim of Russian policy be—besides, of course, the welfare of the Russian people? (Even Stalin used that to justify his actions.) Should it be a restoration of our military superpower status? Should it be the rejection of imperial ambition and concomitantly the emancipation of society in the name of economic, social, and cultural development?

Combining the two is impossible both in practice (since we lack the resources) and in principle (since these are two different tracks, two different social and governmental structures, two vastly different sets of ideals). The Bolsheviks sought to make the state all-powerful, in the name of "labor freely performed by people freely assembled." What they got was forced labor in the Gulag.

Imperial ideas are indeed magnificent:

Immoveable and high
Above the furious Neva
Sits the idol, arm extended,
On a horse of bronze.

. . .

So fearsome is he in the murk!
Such thought upon his brow!
Such strength concealed within!
Such fire in his mount!
Where are you bound, proud steed,
where will those hooves come down?[2]

2

Russian "statists" have always relied on well-coined lines like these to
deflect any questions about ultimate goals, to suggest that their goals
are goals for the ages, goals wrought in marble and bronze—sacrosanct
symbols of empire subject to neither critical nor rational debate.

This ideology cum state religion had proved more than resistant to
social upheaval. Its most amazing incarnation has been, of course, the
Bolshevik one. But the Bolshevik revolution, the most radical in world
history, never even came close to unseating Russia's bronze horseman.
Imperial-state ideals emerged from the fires of revolution both trans-
figured and strengthened.

Writer and monarchist V. V. Shulgin said as much in 1920, when he
so aptly described the essence of the socialist revolution and civil war:
"In summary, against my will, against your will, the Bolsheviks are: one,
restoring Russia's military; two, restoring the natural borders of the
Russian empire; three, preparing the way for the advent of a [new] tsar
and autocrat of all the Russias."[3]

Those words are just as applicable today as they were then. More
and more statists (and who among our currently active politicians would
not hasten to declare himself one?) are solemnly declaring that the first
two points on Shulgin's list are among their top priorities; lately these
are called "maintaining our defense capacity" and "reconstituting" or
"reestablishing" the USSR in some yet undetermined form. And, as

Shulgin notes, if the state focuses on resolving the first two issues, the third one will resolve itself.

Will we see yet another metamorphosis? Another incarnation of the state? In Russia, do democratic evolution and socialist revolution inevitably lead to the same end? Is Russian history indeed programmed, choreographed, so that no matter what the starting point, what the steps, the combinations, the pirouettes along the way, it will inevitably dance its way to the foot of the throne? To the foot of the dictator? Are all efforts by liberals and democrats to change the vector of Russian history doomed from the outset?

I am convinced that they are not—otherwise what would be the point of working in politics at all, of trying to melt the polar ice of "statism" in which the living body of the nation is encased? But at the same time we must be realistic, and acknowledge the possibility of such a turn of events. Most important of all, however, we must remember that what happens tomorrow depends on our efforts.

3

The signs of a new ice age are certainly upon us. Many people who in 1989–91 swore their allegiance to a civil society and democratic ideals are now just as passionately swearing their allegiance to a strong state, to a "firm hand." Yesterday phrases like "rule of law" rolled off their tongues; today the "of law" part seems to have disappeared.

This shift in rhetoric is not so terrible in itself, but it is symptomatic. A religion of the state is again being imposed on the nation. It is hard not to notice this incremental "molecular" regeneration of official authority, which is in fact a return to the old, "normal" way of doing things.

The issue is all the more complex because here we have a not entirely disinterested play on words, a substitution of one concept for another. Really, what responsible politician would oppose the building of an efficient, capable government, a strong and effective state? And is there any doubt that the Russian state is currently neither strong, nor efficient, nor capable of action?

Of course Russia must have efficient, capable government. It must be a working state. In that sense I am certainly a statist, and that is precisely why I stand in categorical opposition to the "statists" spoken of above. To avoid any misinterpretation, let me explain.

The issue comes down to the goals and priorities of the state, or in essence to what the state must be, and must do. If modernizing the country and clearing the socioeconomic ground for the development of a modern society is the priority, then the state's obligation is relatively clear-cut and limited.

The state's obligation is to overcome "statism" in all its forms and gradations; the state must ensure the sanctity of private property by making a clear separation between property ownership and official authority. It must relinquish its position as chief property owner of the nation, as axis of all economic relations. It must actively fight inflation, encourage both foreign and domestic investment, and energetically pursue an antimonopoly policy.

It must concern itself with environmental protection, with public health, with the development of science and culture. It must concern itself with the poor and the disabled.

One of the government's most crucial tasks today is to fight against the frightening upsurge in street crime, and the rise of the mafia, which seems to be defining economic process in Russia today—twisting the market's arm.

The state itself must also give up its own "extortion racket"—that is, curb its appetite for tax revenues. This is a perfectly achievable goal if the state can only give up its role as chief investor in the Russian economy.

Finally, Russia must undertake a reasonable, considered defense policy, which involves, among other things, conversion of the military-industrial complex—that great bulwark of state ownership—to civilian use. This means reducing armed forces to a size based on the country's needs rather than the generals'.

This is one "statist" approach: effective, affordable government capable of fostering dynamic social development in the coming century. This approach presumes an ideology to match: secularization of the state, a rational "Western" attitude toward the state, a rejection of the religion of the state.

But if the priority is to "restore military greatness," to "maintain a great-power image at any cost," "to restore our natural borders," to "recover the territory of the former USSR," then an entirely different approach is required.

Obviously, such a priority is hard to justify in rational terms. We can hardly claim that we as a nation, as a people, are suffocating for lack of *Lebensraum,* or that we are insufficiently armed.

Here, a priori, we have an irrational, spiritual relationship to government—statism as an official religion. None of this would be possible without officially sanctioned xenophobia or without the invention of some new enemy of the state, whether foreign, domestic, or both.

Further, this policy obviously presupposes (and its ideology fully supports) a drastic reduction of political, economic, and civil rights in favor of an expansion of state power and revenue, yet another mass mobilization of society's resources to resolve the problems of empire. I am convinced that such a course of action will lead straight to disaster, to the collapse of an already exhausted nation and the state that sits atop it. What worked in the 1920s and 1930s will not work on the eve of the millennium. Territorial expansion is an exchange of space for time: an extension of the physical dimensions of an empire at the cost of historic regression, a return to archaic (indeed, feudal-autocratic) forms of rule. And this, for Russia, is the road to ruin.

We can say the same about the economy. Pursuing "imperial" projects would mean that we reinforce the entire military-industrial complex (at whose cost, with what resources?) and thus the whole state-managed economic sector that revolves around it.

From an economic perspective, this is obviously the road to nowhere. Can it be that our "statists" do not see that *they themselves* are the worst enemies of the Russian state and the Russian nation?

The answer lies in turning from big words and bigger promises, from marble verses and iron rhetoric, to everyday prose, to realism, to the affairs of a real state run by real people.

4

Somehow "the bronze, the flying horseman" all too quickly freezes into the statue of the Gogol-style town mayor, and the motto "L'état surtout" becomes "L'état, c'est moi." Today what we have are state interests rather than state ideals, which means not interests of state but the interests of our ever insatiable "statists."

The state consists of property owned by a bureaucracy. As I have tried to demonstrate, Marx's equation has described the situation rather precisely. However, as Russia enters a new era of primitive capital accumulation, as she has managed, with great difficulty, to shift course by at least a few degrees in the direction of democratic and market-oriented privatization, the real ideals of our statists and patriots are all too transparent. What concerns them is not "socialism," not "empire," not "military might." These are just words. What these people want is far more prosaic. They want to reinstate the bureaucratic market, to perpetuate a pseudostate economy in which their private capital functions as state capital, with all the rights and privileges accruing thereto.

On one hand, the nomenklatura are not about to give up the gains made during nomenklatura privatization. Total state monopoly on property is dead and gone, and it is hardly in the interests of the bureaucracy to revive it. They are not about to renationalize what they've personalized, not about to take their winnings and dump them back into the common pot.

On the other, a true system of private ownership has yet to develop. And it is not in the interest of today's Russian bureaucracy to establish one.

So here we have our own Scylla and Charybdis, as the Russian ship of state, all flags flying and trumpets sounding, steers a course dangerously close to both. The bureaucracy's goal is to salvage, to maintain our "half-finished" system of property relations. The indeterminate nature of these relations allows the bureaucracy to remain unaccountable for property that officially belongs to no one, while continuing to control it and profit from this property as if it were their own—true parasitic imperialism. For the protection, the growth, the perpetuation of this order, the bureaucracy needs a strong state. As the old Russian proverb says, "The state gets fat and stout while the people do without."

The logic behind such political behavior is exceedingly simple. Between 1989 and 1991 this very bureaucracy had opposed any augmentation of state authority. Most bureaucrats were democrats—or almost democrats, at least. Why? Because a certain easing off of the screws would allow them to "privatize" their authority, to become owners instead of administrators. But now that process is over. Everything once up for grabs has already been grabbed. The bureaucracy's needs have changed and now it wants strong government; now "statism" is once again in favor.

These are the interests that underlie Russia's new statism. Lately a particular sort of bureaucrat, an exceedingly cynical and predatory type, has been calling the tune. It is not a matter of specific people or personalities, but of the social climate in today's Russia. Corruption is Russia's ancient and perhaps eternal scourge. As Nikolai Gogol once wrote:

> The dishonorable business of taking bribes has become a necessity, a requirement even for people never born to be dishonest. . . . [W]e must save our country. . . . which is perishing not at the hands of invading hordes, but by our own hands, ours alone: alongside lawful government another type of governing has taken shape, one much stronger than its lawful equivalent. Terms are set, everything has its price, and everyone knows the prices.

Gogol goes on to explain why administrative-bureaucratic efforts to fight corruption proved ineffective: "And no ruler, even if he be wiser than all lawgivers and rulers together, is powerful enough to set these things right, however he might seek to curb the power of evil officials by setting other officials over them."[4]

But Gogol was overstating the matter: Russia might have been in critical condition in Gogol's day, even close to death. But she didn't die. She continued to grow and develop in spite of the corruption within. In our day the situation is qualitatively different; the mafia is everywhere. The current alliance between organized crime and official corruption is capable of producing a terrible hybrid quite unlike anything Russia has ever seen before—an all-powerful, all-criminal state, a true beast of the apocalypse. We should not forget that a bureaucrat is potentially much more corruptible than is a businessman. A businessman can actually get rich honestly, if the system allows him to. The only way for a bureaucrat to become rich is to become dishonest. A bureaucratic organization (an enforcement system, a punitive system) can easily become a mafia. The chief difference lies in their purpose, their goals.

It is obvious what sort of state will take shape if we allow ourselves to be guided by today's "statist" ideals. It will be corrupt, criminal, colonialist. Society will become the colony of the terrible state, the state a colony of the foreign and domestic mafia that has permeated every pore of the bureaucratic apparatus. Russia herself will become a colony of private firms, a source of raw materials for advanced societies, for "open societies and their companies."

And this would be a perfectly natural outcome, because a "strong state," in our usual understanding of the word (i.e., a large and virtually omnipotent bureaucracy) means the following.

It means no equal protection under the law for private property or property rights. To the contrary: one's claim to property would be contingent on one's place in the bureaucratic hierarchy, which means that honest, energetic people have little hope of advancement on their own. It means an economy where monopoly rules, where the market trades in bribes—a modern version of Russia's traditional bureaucratic exchange.

It means that the only way to support "selected" industries (read here banking and industry cronies) and upper level officials (the ever-growing ranks of military and security personnel) is to print more and more money, to create inflation.

It means that our "economic pyramids"—our outdated and inefficient monuments to monopoly—will remain standing.

It means that our taxes will remain inordinately high. This, combined with government racketeering (bribes to state officials), guarantees that small and medium business, which is the most dynamic part of any capitalist economy, the "incubator" for the middle class, will never even get off the ground.

It means that the Russian economy will be closed to most of the world, to anyone not considered a "friend of the firm."

I believe that many of our current officials are cynical enough to understand precisely what sort of "strong government" they are building. They harbor no hope of reviving our military empire any time soon; they have no real desire to do so. In fact, imperial ideals have been devalued among great-power enthusiasts no less than among democrats. The difference is that while democrats may have traded these ideals for other, equally general and abstract ones, Russian imperialists simply have never had any ideals at all. Their imperial two-headed eagle is the golden calf in disguise. They plan to grow fat on its meat—on behalf of, in the name of, at the cost of, the Russian state.

Our statists have neither a great plan nor a clear strategy for building that state, or its economy. This absence of any real goal or real faith in their own passionately proclaimed goals is now coming back to haunt them. If the only goal is to maintain the ambiguous status quo, to force the country to continue swinging back and forth between state and private ownership, the mediocre "decadents of statism" are the only ones to do it.

To some degree our current situation resembles that of late 1991, although we are in somewhat better shape at the moment. Back then the ruling bureaucracy (statists "by office") refrained from any radical moves because backstage wheeling and dealing, "covert privatization," suited their purposes. It was the radical-democratic parties ("antistatists," in current political parlance) who demonstrated political will, who led the charge.

So it is today. Our "official statists" are quite happy to run in place, while the only people with any real strategy, with any real political or economic policy to offer are the liberals, the democrats.

The debate over "socialist state" versus "classic capitalism" is purely academic. Neither Hayek nor Keynes had Russia's current nomenklatura-Asiatic-mafioso state in mind when they worked out their theories. Only if and when we change the system, if and when we lay at least the foundations of a Western society will this choice apply.

The privatization of state authority, the collapse of a bureacratic empire that has been corroded, consumed from within by a bureaucratic oligarchy, is the inevitable end to any "Eastern" empire. It marks the end of the spiral, the cycle. We must do all we can to ensure that the Bolshevik cycle is the last such in Russian history, that it does not begin again. Russia today has a unique opportunity to change her entire historical orientation, her social, political, economic orientation, to become a republic in the Western sense of that term.

In this century, Russian society has traveled a huge and tragic circle, gone round Solzhenitsyn's "red wheel" from an almost normal market economy (1900–1914) to a militarized state-capitalist economy with markets and predominantly private property ownership (1921–29) to a totalitarian economy and total elimination of markets and private ownership (1929–53).[5]

Those years marked the ascent, and the peak of communism. But then came the second half of the century, and the descent from those dizzying heights. There was a certain symmetry between the road up and the road down: the latter went from a state-monopoly economy (imperialism) with a semi-legal market and "shadow" property (1953–85) to a state-capitalist economy, first in the guise of pseudostate relations, then gradually led to overt private ownership and the legitimization of the bureaucratic market (1985–91).

In 1992 we began to move toward "normal" markets and legitimate private property.

But always, at the center of this whirl of activity, there lay a tremendously powerful magnet—the bureaucratic state. Its force field has always determined the trajectory of Russian history, has deformed the face of Russia; it has consumed and destroyed its own society and destroyed itself in the process.

Will we be able, at last, to break free of this orbit? This is the main question upon which the future of Russia depends.

5

We are entering the twenty-first century. Western society is far from ideal. It is selfish, self-absorbed, consumed with quite serious problems of its own: a predominantly "northern orientation," overpopulation (which has for the first time since Malthus become a real threat), and an environmental crisis. One problem with capitalism is that it grows too far too fast. It is stable only when it is enjoying a boom, as new demand arises and is satisfied.

The West is neither our enemy nor our patron. We must solve our own problems, and if we do not, the rest of the world will hardly be too concerned about the collapse of a great civilization.

We have quite a few of them to solve.

We have nineteenth-century problems (the creation of a rule of law), early twentieth-century problems (eradication of the vestiges of social and industrial feudalism), plus all the late twentieth-century ones (the abrupt demonopolization of the economy, the war against fascism and other extremist forms of self-destructive nationalism). All these dog us as we enter the twenty-first century.

We also have our own uniquely Russian problems: the creation a middle class, for one; legal and popular recognition of legitimate private ownership.

And we must solve all these simultaneously. Taking them one at a time is not an option, because the world will not wait, and history will make no allowances for us. Our problems run the gamut from investment (private or state) to overall social and political policy and ideology.

So—do we do business as usual? Or do we break the circuit, cut the cord between government office and property ownership?

Shall we deify the state, or shall we secularize it, separate it from the pseudochurch of "statism"?

These are the global and historical alternatives facing Russia; they are also political alternatives for today.

If our country begins yet another cycle of privatization of authority and office, it will shut itself off from the First World. If we can open up this socioeconomic space, if we can let liberal democratic evolution take its course, then Russia will have every chance in the world to take its rightful place among twenty-first-century civilizations.

For some, a statist approach is synonymous with maintaining bureaucratic institutions, maintaining their wealth and power. For others it means simply keeping the nation intact. To do so we must transform it, and we must apply all our political will to this task.

We must remove the shards of the old system from the new body politic. The old system has borne many names: Autocracy, Internationalism, Communism, National Bolshevism. Lately it has been trying

"Great Power" on for size. But its essence has always been the same: self-serving and predatory bureaucratic rule, self-serving demagoguery.

I have already written that I consider myself and my cohorts true statists, and true patriots. I say so for one simple reason: our chief aim is to find long-term solutions, to see market reforms through to their end, to build a stable, dynamic, increasingly prosperous Western style society in Russia.

When I say Western style society, I am not talking about naive notions of "universal culture." But one principle does seem to me to be truly universal, and quite fitting for Russia, even though it was first formulated by an American named Thomas Jefferson: "We hold these Truths to be self-evident, that all Men are created equal, that they are endowed by their Creator with certain unalienable Rights, that among these are Life, Liberty, and the pursuit of Happiness."

August–September 1994
Moscow

Notes

Preface to the English-Language Edition

1. The title of the book is a play on *State and Revolution,* one of Vladimir Ilyich Lenin's most famous works. Written on the eve of October 1917, *State and Revolution* was intended to be a theoretical justification for seizure of power by the proletariat, and a summary of Marxist views on the essence of the state and the means by which it might be transformed, chief among which was revolution.

2. The allusion is to philosopher Aleksandr Zinoviev's 1974 novel *The Yawning Heights (Ziyayushchie vysoty),* a biting satire on the Soviet system. The title itself is a play on "the shining *[siyayushchie]* heights of Communism," a long-standing Soviet cliché.

3. The term *nomenklatura* refers to the list of state officials who, in the Soviet era, enjoyed a wide range of privileges commensurate to their place in the state hierarchy. "Nomenklatura privatization" and "nomenklatura capitalism" were terms widely used in the Russian press in the 1990s, and reflect the close involvement (too close, in the opinion of many Russians) of the former elite in postsocialist privatization.

1. Two Civilizations

1. The author is referring to *Postizhenie istorii,* a 1991 Russian edition of British historian Arnold Toynbee's *A Study of History,* published in twelve volumes between 1934 and 1961.

2. K. Marx and F. Engels, *Sochineniya (Works),* 2d ed., vol. 25 part 1, p. 354.

3. Leonid Vasiliev, *Istoriya Vostoka (A History of the East)* (Moscow, 1993) vol. 1, part 1, p. 17.

4. Ibid.

5. The Zhou dynasty of China lasted from 1027 to 221 B.C., but in 771

the Zhou court was sacked by invaders, which brought about a division of the kingdom and eventual decline. The latter part of the Zhou era is known as the Warring States or Warring Kingdoms Period (475–221 B.C.). "Fujiwara Japan" refers to the ninth–twelfth centuries of the Heian Period, when the Fujiwara family dominated the political scene.

6. From John Stuart Mill's *Principles of Political Economy* (New York: D. Appleton and Co., 1872), vol.1, book 2, p. 307. The complete sentence reads: "Custom is the most powerful protector of the weak against the strong; their sole protector where there are no laws or government adequate to the purpose."

7. From *Igry obmena,* the 1988 Russian translation of Fernand Braudel's *Jeux de L'Echange* (1979), 2: 610, published in English as *The Wheels of Commerce: Civilization and Capitalism 15th–18th Century.*

8. The Rzeczpospolita Polska to which the author refers is the Polish-Lithuanian Commonwealth that took shape after the 1569 Union of Lublin and lasted into the eighteenth century. The Rzeczpospolita was ruled by a king elected by an assembly of nobles, and eventually fell to its neighbors (Russia, Prussia, and Austro-Hungary) in a series of partitions, the last of which took place in 1795.

9. From the Russian translation of *The Communist Manifesto.* In Marx and Engels, *Sochineniya,* 4:429, 480.

10. From the Russian translation of H. G. Wells's *Russia in the Shadows (Rossiya vo mgle)* (Moscow, 1970), pp. 62–63.

11. Gaidar is referring to liberal economist Friedrich August Hayek's *The Fatal Conceit: The Errors of Socialism,* first published in 1988 (Chicago: University of Chicago Press; London: Routledge).

12. Bernstein's revisionist theories came under fierce attack by Karl Kautsky, Lenin, and other Marxist theorists. The author here refers to the Russian translation of Bernstein's book, which was published in St. Petersburg in 1891.

13. The author here refers to the Russian translation of Keynes's book published as part of the series *Antologiya ekonomicheskoi klassiki (An Anthology of Classics in Economics)* (Moscow, 1993).

14. The Congress of People's Deputies was a two-tier legislative body, a Soviet institution that continued to exist through the first several years of democratic Russia. Deputies were chosen in a general election; they then, from their own ranks, elected what was essentially the real parliament—the Supreme Soviet. The Congress met periodically to decide basic constitutional

issues, while the Supreme Soviet was permanently in session, its chief function being to draft and pass legislation. During the tumultuous years of Gorbachev's perestroika, the Congress of People's Deputies was the center of political life in the country. Later, the Fifth Congress of People's Deputies of the Russian Federation was to support President Boris Yeltsin's economic reform program almost unanimously, only to begin opposing it fiercely when the first difficulties involved in reform became clear. A tug-of-war followed: the government was attempting to implement market reforms while the populist parliament was doing everything it could to stymie them. After ratification of the 1993 Constitution of the Russian Federation, the Congress of People's Deputies and the Supreme Soviet were replaced by a bicameral legislature consisting of the Federal Assembly (which included the Council of the Federation) and the State Duma. Ruslan Imranovich Khasbulatov, an economist by profession, was one of the most outspoken opponents of economic reform. He served as speaker of the Supreme Soviet until late 1993, when Yeltsin dissolved the parliament and ordered the so-called Siege of the White House, the parliament building which Khasbulatov and opposition deputies refused to leave. For a more detailed account, see the author's *Days of Defeat and Victory* (Seattle and London: University of Washington Press, 2000).

15. "I would like to once again remind the reader that 'Eastern,' 'Asiatic,' 'Western,' and 'European' are being applied as purely political-economic categories, not as geographical or ethnic ones. Japan, for example, would here be considered 'Western,' while Cuba or Haiti would be 'Eastern' in form."—Ye. G.

2. A Catch-up Civilization

1. The line is from "The Serpent Tugarin," a poem written in 1867 by popular poet and playwright Aleksei Konstantinovich Tolstoy (1817–75). Debate over the effects of the Mongol conquest (roughly 1240–1480) and its ultimate influence on Russian government and society has persisted over centuries, and many contemporary Russian historians still consider the "Tatar yoke" the main reason behind Russia's long-standing inability to "catch up" to her European neighbors.

2. See works by historian Nikolai Pavlovich Pavlov-Silvansky (1869–1908) for a brilliant overview of the period. These include *Feodalizm v drevnei Rusi (Feudalism in Ancient Rus')* and *Feodalizm v udel'noi Rusi (Feudalism in Appanage Rus')*, published in 1907 and 1910 respectively.

3. Ivan III reigned as Grand Prince of Moscow from 1462 to 1505, his son Vasily III from 1505 to 1533, and his grandson Ivan IV (better known in the West as Ivan the Terrible) from 1533 to 1584. Under Ivan III, the core of a Russian state began to take shape around Moscow; under Vasily III, after the Mongols had suffered a number of defeats, Muscovy was finally unified. Ivan IV, "prince of all the Russias," conquered the Kazan and Astrakhan khanates in 1547 and 1556, and was the first to take the title of tsar.

4. A *pomestye* was land granted and held on condition of service, as opposed to a *votchina*—"patrimonial" lands belonging to clans or families. The *pomestye* system, which existed from the fifteenth to the eighteenth centuries, did not allow grantees to sell or trade the land, nor to leave it to their heirs.

5. St. George's Day (Yuriev den'): one day each year, after the harvest, Russian serfs traditionally had the right to change masters. This right was abolished in 1592. The ukaz of 1597 declared that any runaway serf caught within five years of escape could be returned to his or her owner.

6. Suleiman the Magnificent ruled the Ottoman Empire from 1520 until 1566; Abbas I (Abbas the Great) was shah of Persia from 1587 until 1628.

7. From Aleksandr Solzhenitsyn's essay "Repentance and Self-Limitation in the Life of the Nation" ("Raskayanie i samoogranichenie kak kategorii natsional'noi zhizni"), written for the collection *From under the Rubble (Iz pod glyb)* in 1972 and 1973.

8. Philosopher and belletrist Nikolai Berdiaev (1874–1948) wrote his *Sud'ba Rossii (The Destiny of Russia)* in 1918, roughly four years before he and a large number of writers and intellectuals were exiled.

9. The Livonian War ran from 1558 to 1583 on the northwestern borders of Muscovy, where Russia faced threats from the Livonian Order, Sweden, and Poland-Lithuania. Despite early successes, and the disbanding of the Livonian Order in 1561, Russia did not achieve one of her chief goals—establishing a port on the Baltic Sea.

10. *Krugovaya poruka* was the collective responsibility of the peasant commune, or *obshchina*, for taxes paid to the state. The commune was also responsible for providing recruits to the army. Leaving the commune was difficult, if not impossible, even after serfdom was abolished in 1861, when the commune remained as an administrative structure on the village level. After the Stolypin reforms of 1906, the institution began to collapse. This helped stimulate the development of capitalism in Russia. When the Communists came to power, however, they made use of long-standing village tradition to further their own campaign for total collectivization of the rural economy.

11. Catherine's *Nakaz*, or *Instruction*, was prepared for a legislative commission she had called in 1766 to codify Russian law, something which had not been done since 1649. Inspired by Montesquieu's *L'esprit des lois*, as well as by other Enlightenment thinkers and their works, she composed what at the time seemed a remarkably liberal document. Yet while it expressed indignation over serfdom in general, it was not a call to abolish it: it merely expressed the hope that masters would not abuse their serfs.

12. Peter III was deposed in a 1762 palace coup led by his wife, Catherine II, and her supporters in the court. He was killed soon after. Peter and Catherine's son Pavel I came to the throne only after his mother's death in 1796, and was himself killed in a palace coup in 1801.

13. "Black-plow" peasants *(chernososhnye krest'yane)* were not serfs but freemen who worked communal lands and bore certain feudal obligations.

14. Vyacheslav Konstantinovich Plehve served as Minister of Internal Affairs and Chief of Gendarmes from 1902 until 1904, when he was assassinated. Sergei Yulievich Witte became Minister of Finance in 1892; he headed the Cabinet (later the Council) of Ministers in 1903. He was soon dismissed, most likely over disagreement with Nikolai II's Far Eastern policy. Recalled in 1905 to negotiate the treaty ending the disastrous Russo-Japanese War of 1905–6, Witte also developed the basic planks in what would eventually become Stolypin's agrarian reform platform. Pyotr Arkadyevich Stolypin was known both for his sweeping reform program and his severity in dealing with revolutionaries. He served as Minister of Internal Affairs, then chief cabinet minister from 1906 until 1911, when he was assassinated.

15. Plehve's "credo" is taken from V. V. Leontovich's *Istoriya liberalizma v Rossii, 1762–1914 (A History of Russian Liberalism, 1762–1914)* (Paris, 1980), p. 239.

16. Ibid., p. 294.

17. Statistics from P. A. Khromov, *Ekonomicheskoe razvitie Rossii v XIX–XX vekakh, 1800–1917 (Russian Economic Development in the 19th and 20th Centuries, 1800–1917)* (Moscow, 1950).

18. Ivan Alekseevich Vyshnegradsky, prominent scholar and member of the St. Petersburg Academy of Sciences, began moving out of academics and teaching in the late 1870s, as he became more and more involved in public service. As Minister of Finances (1888–92) he managed to balance the budget, increase gold reserves, and strengthen the exchange value of the paper ruble.

19. Statistics from S. N. Prokopovich's *Opyt ischisleniya narodnogo dokhoda po 50 guberniyam (An Attempt to Calculate National Income Based on 50 Provinces),*

published in Moscow in 1918. According to Prokopovich, per capita income in Russia rose by 50 percent between 1894 and 1913. During that same period, Germany saw an increase of 58 percent, France 52 percent, Italy 121 percent.

3. The Three Sources and Three Components of Bolshevism

1. Like the title of the book, the title of this chapter alludes to one of Lenin's most famous works. In this case it is "The Three Sources and Three Components of Marxism," first published in the August 1913 issue of the Bolshevik monthly *Prosveshchenie (Enlightenment).*

2. Yevgeny Shvarts (1896–1958) wrote his play *Drakon: Skazka v trekh deistviyakh (The Dragon: A Fairy Tale in Three Acts)* during the Second World War, but the play was not performed until 1962, during the Thaw. It was widely perceived as a veiled commentary on Stalinism—the first of many to come.

3. Grigory Melekhov, the central figure in Sholokhov's 1928 novel *The Quiet Don,* is a young Cossack who, after serving in the tsarist cavalry on the Russian-German front in World War I, moves back and forth between the Whites and the Reds in Russia's civil war, never at ease in either camp. At the end of the novel, exhausted both morally and physically by seven years of fighting, he stands on the threshold of his ruined house and contemplates what this new life may bring.

4. *Pugachevshchina* refers to the nature of the rebellion led by Cossack Emelian Pugachev in 1773 and 1774. A chaotic, vengeful, and brutal popular revolt aimed at redressing social wrongs by wiping out the existing order, it ran its course rather quickly, but left deep marks on Russian society.

5. "Therefore it is ridiculous to reduce the Russian revolution to a matter of German gold; far more serious and complex things were at work here. And dreams of world revolution were not entirely the ravings of fanatics; the war was indeed a world war, and there were indeed people throughout Europe who felt angry and betrayed, who had 'abolished God' (the practical result of Marx's theoretical call to 'storm the heaven'). . . . Europe was balanced on a razor's edge. If Russia's price for a catastrophic war and the frustration of an entire generation was Bolshevism, other nations paid their price as well, with the rise of Fascism and Nazism. This 'lost generation' succumbed to the temptations of totalitarianism, and led the liberal world (which had deceived it, betrayed it) to the very edge of rain. This was, as Hitler biographer Joachim Fest put it, 'the most powerful trend of the times,

the sign under which the first half of the century lived.' The horror of the First World War did not end in Compiègne Forest on November 11, 1918; it merely took a breather. The evil energy loosed by that war continued to do its work until 8 May 1945."—Ye. G.

The German gold to which the author refers is the subsidy given Lenin by the German government when he slipped back into Russia in a sealed train car on the eve of the Revolution.

6. During the Stalinist purges of the late 1930s, most cases were reviewed by *osobye soveshchaniya*—"special commissions" or "special boards" of the NKVD. They dispensed with such legal formalities as evidence and defense counsel, and imposed sentences ranging from several years in labor camps to the death penalty.

7. V. I. Lenin, *Polnoe sobranie sochinenii (Complete Works)*, vol. 30, p. 163.

8. Ibid., 23:361.

9. Ibid., 34:193.

10. Ibid., 30:347. "Communism = Soviet rule + nationwide electrification" was a formula that Lenin used to promote rural electrification, a development plan designed under the tsar but implemented under the Bolsheviks in the early 1920s.

11. Ibid., 34:156.

12. Ibid., 34:161.

13. The author is referring to Karl Kautsky (1854–1938) and Rudolf Hilferding (1877–1941), German Social Democrats who opposed revisionist Marxists such as Bernstein but were not necessarily sympathetic to Lenin and the Bolsheviks. Jack London's *The Iron Heel*, a futuristic tale of capitalism and tyranny, was first published by Macmillan in 1908 and subsequently translated into Russian.

14. Lenin, *Polnoe sobranie sochinenii*, 32:83.

15. Ibid., 34:192.

16. These lines are from Voloshin's poem "Severovostok" ("Northeast"), written at his home in Koktebel in 1920 as the Red Army was advancing into the Crimea. The names he mentions are among the most notorious in Russian history: Malyuta Skuratov was Ivan the Terrible's chief henchman; General Aleksei Arachkeev was prime minister during the second half of Aleksandr I's reign. Voloshin's use of archaic terms to describe both past and current events suggests the ongoing connection between Russia's past and present. The epigraph to the poem is supposedly addressed to Attila the Hun by St. Loup, Archbishop of Troyes: "May your arrival be blessed, Scourge of God Whom I serve. I cannot stop you."

17. Ugrium-Burcheev is the eponymous bully-mayor depicted by Mikhail Saltykov-Shchedrin (1826–89) in his classic 1870 novel *Istoriya odnogo goroda (History of a Town)*, a grotesque satire on Russian officialdom.

18. From Leontiev's *Pis'ma k A. Gubastovu (Letters to A. Gubastov)*, in *Russkoe obozrenie (Russian Review)*, no. 5, 1897.

19. Semyon Lyudvigovich Frank (1877–1950) was a philosopher and bel-letrist, a one-time Marxist who contributed to the famous 1909 essay collection *Landmarks (Vekhi)*. He was exiled in 1922. Mikhail Zoshchenko (1895–1958) and Andrei Platonov (1899–1951) were writers and satirists whose protagonists were the half-educated peasants and proletarians who now held sway, whose speech was a bizarre combination of earthy idiom and mangled officialese.

4. Property, the Nomenklatura, and Nomenklatura Property

1. Marx and Engels, *Sochineniya*, 1:438, 272.

2. From Heller and Nekrich's *Utopia in Power (Utopiya u vlasti)* (London, 1986).

3. Thermidor was the eleventh month in the calendar of French Revolution. On 9 Thermidor (July 27, 1794) Robespierre and his fellow Jacobins were overthrown by the combined forces of old bourgeoisie and the nouveaux riches.

4. Ilya Ehrenburg (1891–1967), journalist and novelist, dabbled in experimental and satirical prose in the 1920s, covered the Spanish Civil War and World War II, and in 1954 wrote *The Thaw*, the novel that gave an era its name. His actual term here is a virtually unpronounceable acronym: "usovkom-chelov," for "usovershenstvovannyi kommunisticheskii chelovek" or "perfect Communist person."

5. In Mikhail Bulgakov's tremendously popular novel *The Master and Margarita* (written in the late 1930s but not published until 1967, long after the author's death), the Devil comes down to Moscow. In his guise as Woland, a "foreign consultant" with an entourage of outrageous assistants, he wreaks havoc on a populace that bears very little resemblance to the new Soviet ideal.

6. L. Trotsky, *Moya zhizn: Opyt avtobiografii (My Life: An Essay in Autobiography)* (Moscow, 1991), pp. 477–79.

7. The "Party limit" established shortly after the revolution (for both democratic and propaganda reasons) was a salary-and-privileges cap on what Party members in government service could receive. Government servants

who were not Party members were not subject to this cap, but as time went on, there were fewer and fewer of them to be found.

8. L. Trotsky, *Predannaya revolyutsiya (The Revolution Betrayed)* (Moscow, 1991), p. 210.

9. In 1956 Milovan Djilas, originally a cohort of Josip Broz Tito and a prominent figure in Yugoslav politics, published his book *The New Class,* a highly critical and influential study of the Communist oligarchy.

10. The refrain is from poet Vladimir Mayakovsky's famous "Levyi marsh" ("Left March"), written in 1918.

11. *Landmarks (Vekhi)* was a collection of seven essays written by prominent left-leaning intellectuals, some former Marxists, including Pyotr Struve, Nikolai Berdiaev, Sergei Bulgakov, and Semyon Frank. It was an attack on Marxism and the radical intelligentsia. *Changing the Landmarks (Smena vekh)* was a pro-Bolshevik collection, and while it took its name from the earlier book, it was not a reply to it.

12. From Czech playwright and prose writer Karel Čapek's *War with the Newts,* published in Russian in 1959.

13. Translated from the Russian edition of José Ortega y Gasset's *Revolt of the Masses* (New York, 1954).

14. Boris Souvarine (1895–1984) was a founding member of the Communist Party of France. Prolific essayist and author of one of the first biographies of Stalin (1935), he was highly critical of the imperial ambitions of the Soviet state.

15. "Camp dust" refers to notorious KGB head Lavrenty Beria's preferred form of threat when interrogating prisoners: " . . . sotru v lagernuyu pyl!" (I'll grind you into camp dust!")

16. A. S. Chernyaev, *Shest' let s Gorbachevym: Po dnevnikovym zapiskam (Six Years with Gorbachev: Notes from a Diary)* (Moscow, 1998), p. 95.

17. Vitaly Naishul is a prominent Moscow economist, director of the Institute of National Model Economics. The quote is from his article "The Highest and Last Stage of Socialism" ("Vysshaya i poslednyaya stadiya sotsializma") in *Sinking into the Quagmire (Pogruzhenie v tryasinu)* (Moscow, 1991).

18. "The poet" is Nikolai Gumilyov, and these are the last lines from his 1921 poem "Slovo" ("Word"). Husband of Anna Akhmatova and himself a leading figure in the intellectual life of prerevolutionary St. Petersburg, Gumilyov was shot by Soviet authorities in 1921, ostensibly for involvement in a counterrevolutionary plot.

19. Aleksandr Solzhenitsyn's phrase "to not live a lie" *(zhit' ne po lzhi),* intended as a watchword for "ideological disobedience" (analogous to civil

disobedience), was also the title of an article he wrote in late 1973. He had planned to publish this article along with his "Letter to Soviet Leaders," but the two were eventually published separately. The call to strip off the old ideology is from "Letter," which itself was written in August 1973, sent to the Central Committee, and then published abroad in 1974 both in Russian and in translation.

20. Georgy Arbatov (b. 1923), a prominent figure before and during perestroika, long headed the Russian Academy of Science's Institute of the U.S. and Canada. He has written widely on economics and U.S.–Soviet relations. These remarks are from *Zatyanuvsheesye vyzdorovlenie (The Long Recovery)* (Moscow, 1991).

21. Yuri Vlasov (b. 1935) is a former Olympic medalist and superheavyweight world champion in weightlifting. He has also written a number of books. In the early 1990s he was active in politics, and ran for office on a "patriotic" program that denounced both the Communists and the "Zionist conspiracy" against the Russian people. His 1995 bid for a Duma seat was unsuccessful.

22. Although dissident historian and playwright Andrei Amalrik (1938–80) was off by a few slight years, his extended essay *Will the Soviet Union Survive until 1984?*, a study of the inevitable disintegration of the USSR, has proven prophetic in many ways.

5. Primitive Capital Accumulation

1. Mikhail Zinovievich Yuriev (b. 1959) was one of the first entrepreneurs to establish cooperatives in Moscow in the late 1980s, and has figured prominently in business and politics in post-Soviet Russia. He is quoted from remarks in *Biznesmeny Rossii: 40 let uspekha (Russian Businessmen: 40 Years of Success)* (Moscow, 1994), p. 193.

2. The reference is to Gavriil Popov, chairman of the Moscow City Soviet in 1990–91, mayor of Moscow in 1991–92. A doctor of economics, Popov was a senior professor at Moscow State University from 1963 to 1988, and editor-in-chief of *Voprosy Ekonomiki (Questions of Economics)* from 1988 to 1990. Popov coined the term "administrative-command system."

3. Yu. Larin, "Chastnyi kapital v SSSR" in *Antologiya ekonomicheskoi klassiki* "(Private Capital in the USSR" in *An Anthology of Classics in Economics)*, vol. 2, pp. 440, 446.

4. "Urozhay-90" (urozhay=harvest) was an attempt to stimulate agricultural production and sales to the government. Peasant farmers were to

receive vouchers for hard-to-find imported goods; these goods were to be bought by the government with money from the sale of Russian oil. But although the oil was apparently sold, no goods ever appeared on the shelves.

5. Ye. T. Gaidar, "Russia and Reforms," *Izvestiya*, 19 August 1992.

6. For a more detailed account of privatization, see Gaidar's *Days of Defeat and Victory.*

7. OMON is the acronym for Russian special forces troops under the command of the Ministry of the Interior. They were often used as SWAT teams or for crowd control.

8. The Red Belt is the term used for those regions, most of them in central Russia, that reelected Communists to positions of power after the collapse of the Soviet Union.

9. "Let me quote, without further commentary, a description of socioeconomic order written in 1848. Readers can make their own comparisons between this description and our own history and reality."—Ye. G.

"The government . . . seldom leaves much to the cultivators beyond mere necessaries, and often strips them so bare even of these, that it finds itself obliged, after taking all they have, to lend part of it back to those from whom it has been taken, in order to provide them with seed, and enable them to support life until another harvest. Under the regime in question, though the bulk of the population are ill provided for, the government . . . is enabled . . . to make a show of riches quite out of proportion to the general condition of the society. . . . A large part is distributed among the various functionaries of government, and among objects of the sovereign's favour or caprice. A part is occasionally employed in works of public utility. . . . The insecurity, however, of all possessions in this state of society, induces even the richest purchasers to give a preference to such articles as, being of an imperishable nature, and containing great value in small bulk, are adapted for being concealed or carried off. Gold and jewels, therefore, constitute a large proportion of the wealth of these nations, and many a rich Asiatic carries nearly his whole fortune on his person, or on those of the women of his harem. No one, except the monarch, thinks of investing his wealth in a manner not susceptible of removal.

. . . . This state of society, however, is not destitute of a mercantile class; composed of two divisions, grain dealers and money dealers. The grain dealers do not usually buy grain from the producers, but from the agents of government. . . . The money dealers lend to the unfortunate cultivators, when ruined by bad seasons or fiscal exactions, the means of supporting life and continuing their cultivation, and are repaid with enormous interest at the next harvest; or on a larger scale, they lend to the government, or to those to whom it has granted a portion of the revenue. . . . the commercial operations of both these classes of dealers take place principally upon that part of the produce of the country which forms the revenue of the government. From that revenue their capital is periodically replaced with a profit, and that is also the source from which their original funds have almost always been derived. Such, in its general features, is the economical condition of most of the countries of Asia, as it has been from beyond the commencement of authentic history, and is still, wherever not disturbed by foreign influences." [From J. S. Mill, *Principles of Political Economy:* (1848).]

6. The Choice

1. J. V. Stalin, "O zadachakh khozyaistvennikov" ("On the Tasks Before our Economic Planners"). Address to the All-Union Conference of Industrial Workers, February 4, 1931.

2. Lines from Aleksandr Pushkin's 1833 poem *The Bronze Horseman*, in which the famous statue of Peter the Great comes to life and descends from its pedestal to terrorize a humble clerk.

3. V. V. Shulgin, *Dni, 1920: Zapiski (Days, 1920: Notes)* (Moscow, 1989), p. 517.

4. *Dead Souls*, Part II, Chapter V.

5. The allusion is to Aleksandr Solzhenitsyn's multivolume historical chronicle *Red Wheel*, which so far includes *August 1914* (first published in Russian in 1971, and recently reissued in English) and *November 1916* (published in English in 1999).

Bibliography

Akhmatova, A. A. *Stikhotvoreniya i poemy* (Poems). Leningrad, 1977.

Amalrik, A. A. "Prosushchestvuyet li Sovetskii Soyuz do 1984 goda?" In *Pogruzhenie v tryasinu* (Will the Soviet Union survive until 1984? in *Sinking into the Quagmire*). Moscow, 1991.

Arbatov, G. A. *Zatyanuvsheesye vyzdorovlenie* (The long recovery). Moscow, 1991.

Berdiaev, N. A. *Sud'ba Rossii* (The destiny of Russia). Moscow, 1918.

Biznesmeny Rossii: 40 let uspekha (Russia's Businessmen: 40 years of success). Moscow, 1994.

Blok, A. A. *Stikhotvoreniya, Poemy, Teatr* (Poetry, drama). Vol. 2. Leningrad, 1972.'

Braudel, F. *Igry obmena: Material'naya tsivilizatsiya, ekonomika i kapitalizm* (Les Jeux de l'echange: Civilisation matérielle, économie et capitalisme). Moscow, 1988.

Bulgakov, M. A. *Izbrannoye* (Selected works). Moscow, 1983.

Čapek, K. *Voina s salamandramy. In Sochineniya* (War with the newts, in *Works*, vol. 5). Moscow, 1959.

Djilas, M. *Litso totalitarizma* (The face of totalitarianism). Moscow, 1992.

Fest, Joachim C. *Gitler: Biografiya* (Hitler: a biography, vol. 3). Perm, 1993.

Gaidar, Ye. T. "Rossiya i reformy" (Russia and reforms). *Izvestiya* no. 187, 19 August 1992.

Gogol, N. *Sobranie sochinenii* (Collected works, vol. 5). Moscow, 1991.

Gosudarstvennyi sovet: Stenograficheskii otchet (State council: Minutes). 1909–1910.

Gumilyov, N. S. *Sobranie sochinenii* (Collected works, vol. 2). Moscow, 1991.

Heller, M., and A. Nekrich. *Utopiya u vlasti* (Utopia in power). London, 1986.

Keynes, J. M. *Obshchaya teoriya zanyatosti, protsenta i deneg. In Antologiya ekonomicheskoi klassiki* (The general theory of employment, interest and money in *An Anthology of Classics in Economics*, vol. 2). Moscow, 1993.

Khromov, P. A. *Ekonomicheskoye razvitie Rossii v XIX-XX vekakh, 1800–1917* (Russian economic development in the 19th and 20th centuries, 1800–1917). Moscow, 1950.

Larin, Yu. "Chastnyi kapital v SSSR." In *Antologiya ekonomicheskoi klassiki* (Private capital in the USSR, in *An Anthology of Classics in Economics*, vol. 2).

Lenin. V. I. *Polnoe sobranie sochinenii* (Complete works, vols. 23, 26, 30, 32, 34). Moscow, n.d.

Leontiev. K. N. "Pis'ma k A. Gubastovu." In *Russkoe obozrenie* (Letters to A. Gubastov in *Russian Review*, no. 5, 1897).

Leontovich, V. V. *Istoriya liberalizma v Rossii, 1762–1914* (A history of Russian liberalism, 1762–1914). Paris, 1980.

Lyashenko, P. I. *Istoriya russkogo narodnogo khozyaistva* (A history of Russia's economy). Moscow, 1930.

Marx K., and F. Engels. *Sochineniya* (Works, 2d ed., vols. 1, 4, 25). Moscow, n.d.

Mill, J. S. *Osnovy politicheskoi ekonomiki* (Principles of political economy). Moscow, 1980.

Milyukov, P. N. *Ocherki po istorii russkoi kul'tury* (Sketches in Russian cultural history). St. Petersburg, 1904.

Mizes, L. F. *Byurokratiya, zaplanirovannyi khaos, antikapitalisticheskaya mental'nost'* (Bureaucracy, planned chaos, the anticapitalist mentality). Moscow, 1993.

Montesquieu, C. L. *O dukhe zakonov.* In *Izbranniye proizvedeniya* (Spirit of the laws, in *Selected Works*). Moscow, 1955.

Naishul, V. "Vysshaya i poslednyaya stadiya sotsializma." In *Pogruzhenie v tryasinu* (The highest and last stage of socialism, in *Sinking into the Quagmire*). Moscow, 1991.

Ortega y Gasset, José. *Vosstanie mass* (Revolt of the masses). New York, 1954.

Pavlov-Silvansky, N. P. *Feodalizm v Rossii* (Feudalism in Russia). Moscow, 1988.

Pilnyak, Boris. *Golyi god. Povest' nepogashennoi luny* (The naked year. Tale of the unextinguished moon). Moscow, 1990.

Plekhanov, G. V. *Sochineniya* (*Works*, vol. 15). Moscow and Leningrad, 1926.

Prokopovich, S. N. *Opyt ischisleniya narodnogo dokhoda po 50 guberniyam* (An attempt to calculate national income based on 50 provinces). Moscow, 1918.

Pushkin, A. S. *Izbranniye proizvedeniya* (Selected works, vol. 1). Moscow, 1968.

Sholokhov, M. A. *Tikhii Don* (The quiet don). Moscow, 1953.

Shulgin, V. V. *Dni, 1920, Zapiski* (Days, 1920, notes). Moscow, 1989.

Solzhenitsyn, A. I. "Raskayanie i samoogranichenie kak kategorii natsionalnoi zhizni" in *Iz-pod glyb.* (Repentance and self-limitation in the life of the nation, in *From under the Rubble*). Paris, 1974.

Stalin, I. V. *Voprosy Leninizma* (Problems of Leninism). Moscow, 1953.

Toynbee, A. *Postizhenie istorii* (The study of history). Moscow, 1991.

Trotsky, L. D. *Moya zhizn: opyt avtobiografii* (My life: an essay in autobiography). Moscow, 1991.

———. *Predannaya revolyutsia* (A revolution betrayed). Moscow, 1991.

Ustryalov, N. V. *Pod znakom revolyutsii* (Under the sign of revolution). Harbin, 1925.

Vasiliev, L. S. *Istoriya vostoka* (A history of the east, vol. 1). Moscow, 1993.

Voloshin, M. A. *Sredotochie vsyekh putyei* (The meeting of all roads). Moscow, 1989.

Wells, H. G. *Rossiya vo mgle* (Russia in the shadows). Moscow, 1970.

Index

Yegor Gaidar, one of Russia's first post-Soviet prime ministers and principal architect of its historic transformation to a market economy, is the author of *Days of Defeat and Victory*. Translator **Jane Ann Miller** also translated *Days of Defeat and Victory*.